SISTERS OF THE
REVOLUTIONARIES

Teresa O'Donnell is a harpist and musicologist. She was awarded a Foras Feasa fellowship to pursue doctoral studies at St Patrick's College, DCU, which she completed in 2012; she also lectured there. Her research has been published in a number of journals including the *Journal of Music Research Online* and the *Journal of the Society for Musicology in Ireland*.

Mary Louise O'Donnell is a harpist and author of *Ireland's Harp: The Shaping of Irish Identity, c. 1770–1880* (2014). She has published widely on topics relating to Irish cultural history, semiotics and performance studies. Her research has been published in *Utopian Studies, Éire-Ireland,* the *Journal of the Society for Musicology in Ireland* and *The Encyclopaedia of Music in Ireland*.

SISTERS OF THE
REVOLUTIONARIES

THE STORY OF MARGARET AND MARY BRIGID PEARSE

Teresa and Mary Louise O'Donnell

MERRION
PRESS

First published in 2017 by
Merrion Press
10 George's Street
Newbridge
Co. Kildare
Ireland
www.merrionpress.ie

978-1-78537-107-3 (Paper)
978-1-78537-108-0 (Kindle)
978-1-78537-109-7 (Epub)
978-1-78537-123-3 (PDF)

British Library Cataloguing in Publication Data
An entry can be found on request

Library of Congress Cataloging in Publication Data
An entry can be found on request

Interior design by www.jminfotechindia.com
Typeset in Bembo 11/14.5 pt
Cover design by www.phoenix-graphicdesign.com

Cover front: The Pearse children. Left to right: Willie, Patrick,
Margaret and Mary Brigid.
Cover back: Margaret (left) and Mary Brigid Pearse.
(All cover images courtesy of Pearse Museum at St Enda's/OPW)

Printed in Ireland by SPRINT-print Ltd

CONTENTS

ACKNOWLEDGEMENTS

We are indebted to Brian Crowley, curator of the Pearse Museum, St Enda's, Rathfarnham, who has been very generous with his knowledge and time and provided access to important collections associated with the Pearse family at Kilmainham Gaol (OPW). We would also like to thank him for granting permission to publish material and reproduce images.

Further, we would like to acknowledge the assistance of Sr Alice Aylward of the Holy Faith Sisters Congregational Archives, Glasnevin, Dublin; Brian Kirby, provincial archivist with the Irish Capuchin Provincial Archives; Fr Brian Mulcahy, archivist of the Passionist Community, Mount Argus, Dublin; Sr Marian Bradley, Sr Brenda Thompson and Sr Rose Miriam Gansle of the Sisters of the Incarnate Word and Blessed Sacrament, Texas, USA; Fr Joseph Mallin, Wah Yan Jesuit College, Hong Kong and the McGloughlin and Scarlett families.

Librarians and archivists at the following institutions provided invaluable information for our research: the Central Catholic Library, the National Archives of Ireland, the National Library of Ireland, Pearse Street Library, University College Dublin (Special Collections) and Trinity College, Dublin Library. The witness statements of the Bureau of Military History, an online initiative of the Military Archives and National Archives, also provided important information for our research.

We wish to thank Conor Graham, Fiona Dunne and their colleagues at Merrion Press/Irish Academic Press for all their assistance in the preparation of this book. To our supporting and loving families, Barry, Jon, Kevin, Claire, Maria, Cecilia, Kevin and Isabella, we thank you for your patience and encouragement. Finally, we are indebted to our parents, Terrie and Michael, for their unconditional support and for fostering in us a love of Irish history and culture. This book is dedicated to both of you.

Teresa and Mary Louise O'Donnell
January 2017

Introduction

This book focuses on the lives of Margaret and Mary Brigid Pearse, sisters of Patrick and Willie who were executed for their roles in the Easter Rising of 1916. The Pearse sisters have long been overshadowed by their famous brothers but they too travelled interesting paths in life. Margaret was a teacher, Irish language activist and politician who shared Patrick's educational vision for a bilingual education system and his political vision of an independent Irish nation. Mary Brigid was a musician, teacher, actress and author of short stories, children's stories, and dramas, but did not agree with her family's political activism. Margaret and Mary Brigid never enjoyed a close relationship like Patrick and Willie; however, they both shared a deep affection for their brothers.

The Pearse sisters have been accorded little attention in the biographies of Patrick. Possible explanations for their neglect may be the lack of source material and the perception that they played only a peripheral role in the history of the Pearse family. Yet Margaret and Mary Brigid, along with Willie, played an integral part in the creation of the complex, multifaceted man that was Patrick Pearse. Indeed, Margaret and her mother were largely responsible for contributing to, and perpetuating, the myth or cult of Patrick Pearse after his execution.

Until Róisín Ní Ghairbhí's recent publication on Willie, little was known about his character, his artistic ability or his commitment to Irish cultural movements in the late nineteenth and early twentieth centuries. It seems an opportune time to illuminate the lives of the other Pearse siblings and finally remove them from the shadow of their famous brothers. Unfortunately, there is a dearth of information on Margaret and Mary Brigid. Consequently, to piece together the story of their lives, we have relied heavily on extant correspondence and writings of the two sisters held at the Pearse Archive in Kilmainham Gaol, Patrick Pearse's own writings and letters, in particular his unfinished autobiography, and newspaper articles and references to the sisters in the collections of various archives and museums.

An examination of the lives of Mary Brigid and Margaret provides a new perspective on how Patrick managed to realise so many of his pedagogical and cultural ambitions, namely through the unstinting support of his parents and siblings. One of the recurring themes of this book is the profound influence that the stable and loving home life enjoyed by the Pearse siblings in their childhood had on their adult lives. Their father, James, often wrote of his desire to create a happy home.[1] Patrick, in his autobiography, frequently spoke about his wish to always be 'at home'[2] and Mary Brigid entitled her book *The Home-Life of Pádraig Pearse*. For Patrick, Willie, Margaret and Mary Brigid, their home was the centre of their lives, the foundation on which everything was built and from which everything could be accomplished. To understand any of the Pearse children, particularly Patrick, one must consider the family that nurtured and shaped them.

From their childhood through to adolescence and adulthood, the Pearse siblings supported each other's projects. Mary Brigid and Willie founded the Leinster Stage Society and Margaret assisted in the foundation of Patrick's school, St Enda's/Scoil Éanna, where she taught French and religious studies. The active participation of both sisters in various associations and projects connected with Patrick and Willie was facilitated by the financial security that their father provided for them before his death. The Pearse sisters were from a typical middle-class background; they were well-educated and instilled with the confidence to pursue writing or educational projects, and were not compelled to eke out a living through paid employment. They had the potential to achieve so much, but their lives were transformed after Easter 1916.

The sisters' responses to their brothers' actions contrasted greatly. Margaret described the Rising as 'tragic but glorious'[3] and from 1916 until her death in 1968, she attended State and public ceremonies in honour of her brothers, actively promoted the Irish language, and served as a Fianna Fáil politician. Mary Brigid, who was of a 'delicate' disposition, struggled to come to terms with her brothers' deaths. After the Rising, Mary Brigid opted to steer clear of their political legacy and focus instead on her literary career. She found it difficult, however, to carve out an identity and a career for herself which was separate from her family name.

This book is the first full-length attempt to engage with the lesser-known Pearse siblings and it complements existing research on the Pearse family. The study provides a fascinating insight into Margaret and Mary Brigid's relationships with their brothers, but also the poignant disintegration of their own relationship following the death of their mother in 1932.

Teresa and Mary Louise O'Donnell

January 2017

CHAPTER 1

The Childhood of Margaret and Mary Brigid Pearse

The half-real, half-imagined adventures of a child are fully rounded, perfect, beautiful, often bizarre and humorous, but never ludicrous.[1]

Patrick Pearse

Margaret and Mary Brigid Pearse were the eldest and youngest of four children born to James (1839–1900) and Margaret Pearse (1857–1932). The children were born above their father's business premises at 27 Great Brunswick Street, Dublin (now Pearse Street); Margaret Mary was born on 4 August 1878, Patrick Henry on 19 November 1879, William James on 15 November 1881 and Mary Bridget (later changed to Brigid) on 26 April 1884. All were baptised at St Andrew's Church, Westland Row, Dublin. Personal accounts of Margaret, Mary Brigid and Patrick recall memories of a happy childhood, a close-knit family and a religious upbringing. Margaret wrote, '[o]ur schooldays and youth were very happy with our loving mother and most devoted father. Our pleasures were simple, [and] cultural'.[2]

Their father, James Pearse, was born on 8 December 1839 in Bloomsbury, London, to Mary Ann Thomson, a Unitarian, and

James, a free thinker. James (junior) had two brothers, William and Henry, and, according to the 1851 Census, the Pearse family were then living at Ellis Street, Birmingham. Due to straitened financial circumstances, the three boys worked from an early age and, consequently, received little education. James worked at various jobs, eventually becoming a sculptor's apprentice. He attended drawing classes in the evening and in his leisure time was an avid reader. After serving his apprenticeship, James moved to Dublin *c.*1859–60 to take up the position of foreman for the English architectural sculptor, Charles Harrison, who had premises in Great Brunswick Street. In the mid-nineteenth century, there was a boom in the building of churches in Ireland and a number of English craftsmen worked from premises in Great Brunswick Street, Westland Row and Townsend Street. James, however, retained his links with Birmingham and was recorded in the 1861 Census as being a visitor to the city. He also travelled back to Birmingham to court and eventually marry Emily Susannah Fox on 28 April 1863 at St Thomas' Church, Birmingham.

James and Emily settled in Dublin shortly after their marriage and, in 1864, he commenced a three-year contract with the firm, Earley and Powell, 1 Upper Camden Street, Dublin, who were specialists in stucco work, stained-glass manufacturing, carving and plastering. James and Emily's first child, Mary Emily (known as Emily) was born in 1864 and a son, James Vincent, arrived two years later in 1866. The family converted to Catholicism sometime after James Vincent's birth as two daughters, Agnes Maud (b.1869) and Amy Kathleen (b.1871), were both baptised Catholic. The Pearse family was received into the church in Mount Argus, Dublin, under the guidance of Fr Pius Devine, a Passionist priest and rector who was impressed with the manner in which James and his family undertook the process.[3] It is unclear, however, if the family's conversion was in earnest or merely to increase James's prospect of gaining increased commissions from the Catholic Church. Whatever his motivation, James benefitted from the patronage of the Catholic Church from the early 1870s onwards. He formed a partnership with Patrick J. O'Neill *c.*1873, based at 182 Great Brunswick Street, which lasted until 1875. Although James enjoyed professional success in this period, his personal life was tinged with tragedy. Both Agnes Maud and Amy Kathleen died in infancy and Emily died from a spinal infection at the age of thirty on 26 July 1876.[4] James and Emily's marriage was a not a happy one and he blamed the death of at least one of his daughters on his wife's neglect.

After Emily's death, James, Mary Emily and James Vincent resided at the home of their friend, John Thomas McGloughlin, 5 Parnell Place, Harold's Cross until James married his second wife, Margaret Brady. She was born on 12 February 1857 to Bridget Savage, a celebrated step dancer from Oldcastle, Co. Dublin, and Patrick Brady, a coal factor from Dublin. The Brady family lived in North Clarence Street, Dublin but also had a property at 7 Aldborough Avenue. Margaret and her sister, Catherine (b.1852), received their education at the Daughters of Charity of St Vincent de Paul School, North William Street which was established by the Religious Sisters of Charity in 1825 and later transferred to the Daughters of Charity in 1857. While working as an assistant at a newsagent and post office on Great Brunswick Street, she met James Pearse, a customer who purchased a newspaper every morning on his way to his rented premises at 27 Great Brunswick Street. After the death of his first wife, James had a clear vision for his future happiness. Letters written during his courtship with Margaret emphasised his belief that the creation and sustainment of a loving and secure home environment was the key to achieving true happiness:

> I think it must be a great blessing and consolation to be permitted to pass through this world of change with one who will be all to you at all times, one whom you can turn to when the world frowns. A home in which you can find peace and rest. I believe I could make great efforts to render such a home happy.[5]

James cited Margaret's homeliness as one of her most appealing characteristics. He described her as 'a grand looking woman with dark hair and eyes, no nonsense about her, plump and ... homely yet bright and full of life'.[6] It is unclear exactly when their courtship began, but by the end of 1876, a mere five months after the death of James's wife, they had already met for a number of dates at Bachelor's Walk and the corner of Westmoreland Street and Carlisle Bridge (now O'Connell Bridge). The courtship was not always smooth as is evinced from some of their correspondence housed at the National Library of Ireland. Due to illness, James and Margaret were unable to meet from Christmas 1876 until some time after St Patrick's Day (17 March) 1877. James declared that the more care he took of himself, the worse his condition became.[7] Nevertheless, Margaret's patience was beginning to wane and she expressed doubts about the viability of their relationship and dissatisfaction that she had not met his children. But James was determined to continue their courtship, declaring that Margaret's affection had filled 'a great void in [his] existence.'[8]

After a brief engagement, James and Margaret planned their nuptials for 24 October 1877 at the Church of St Agatha, North William Street, Dublin; she had been baptised there on 16 February 1857. Despite the fact that it was commonplace for widowers with children to remarry and that Margaret's marriage would have been regarded as a good match in terms of social class, Margaret's parents had some reservations about the impending nuptials, in particular, the challenge for Margaret of raising two step-children. To the annoyance of the young couple, they suggested the wedding be delayed by a few weeks. James insisted that Margaret's family were aware of his good character but he accepted that Margaret's parents only had their daughter's interests at heart. He implored Margaret to be patient and to inform her parents 'to save their scolding for' him.[9] The wedding was not postponed and both Patrick and Bridget Brady attended the nuptials. Margaret's sister, Catherine, of 160 Great Brunswick Street, and James's friend, John McGloughlin, acted as their witnesses. By all accounts, the marriage of James and Margaret was a happy one; they set up home (and business) along with Mary Emily and James Vincent in a rented property at 27 Great Brunswick Street, a large building which was sublet to other families.

Eighteen seventy-eight proved to be a productive year for James. He embarked on a ten-year partnership with his foreman, Edmund Sharp, and in August of that year, Margaret gave birth to their first child, Margaret Mary, known as 'wow-wow' and 'Maggie' to her family. Margaret was a precocious, bossy child. She adored her father 'Papa' and was very proud of his achievements. He, in turn, indulged her every whim. Fifteen months after her birth, Patrick Henry was born. Patrick became seriously ill at the age of six months and the family doctor advised that there was a poor prospect of survival; the infant, however, survived. Their half-sister Emily later wrote about Patrick's 'sweet uncomplaining patience' during his illness and she noted that this was part of the young Patrick's gentle nature and natural reserve.[10]

Patrick's earliest recollection of family life was of playing with his sister in the dimly-lit living-room in the basement of their home in Great Brunswick Street and the distinctive sounds of that space:

> the carolling of the black fire-fairy, the ticking of a clock, and the rhythmic tap-tapping which came all day from the workshop. In this tap-tapping there were two distinct notes: one sharp and metallic, which I knew afterwards to be the sound of a chisel against hard marble; the other soft and dull, subsequently to be recognised as the sound of a chisel against Caen stone.[11]

Margaret was delighted to have a younger sibling with whom she could play, but perhaps, more importantly, whom she could 'enlighten'. As the elder sibling, Margaret's opinion invariably prevailed. Patrick recalled, '[s]he insisted that her wisdom and experience were riper than mine, and, by dint of hearing this again and again repeated, I came to believe it and to entertain for her a serious respect.'[12] On one occasion, Margaret encouraged Patrick to cut the tail off a toy horse his father had brought him from London; because the mane and tail of the 'London horse' were made of real horse's hair, Margaret convinced him that it would grow back. When it did not, Patrick soon realised that Margaret was not as wise or knowledgeable as she unfailingly led him to believe.

Margaret and Patrick played happily together as young children but because she was 'both bigger and of a more dominating character',[13] she dictated the content and nature of their playtime, which frequently irked Patrick. She had a particular penchant for re-enacting battles that occasionally resulted in fatalities. Patrick believed that Margaret should take responsibility for burying her own dead, but to his great annoyance, Dobbin, a treasured wooden horse carved by his father, was often commandeered to carry the dead on a solemn journey for burial at Glasnevin Cemetery. These childhood games were simple but fondly remembered. Margaret and Patrick were most content sitting with their parents in the drawing room in front of the fire watching the fire-fairy or playing with their pets, Minnie, the lazy cat who invariably positioned himself at the centre of the hearth, and Gyp, their accident-prone hyperactive dog.

Margaret and Patrick had many adventures in their drawing room in Great Brunswick Street, traversing its floor 'in sleighs, in Roman chariots, in howdahs on the backs of elephants' and bravely travelling into remote corners of the room 'where wild beasts prowled'.[14] The children believed that their toys came to life at night time when silence descended on the household. They imagined that their dolls competed in races on the 'London Horse', that their toy cows grazed under the furniture and that Patrick's white goat climbed the treacherous vertical cliff otherwise known as the Pearse's couch. One night, while Margaret slept, Patrick crept downstairs to observe their toys' nocturnal adventures, alas with no success. Fear of the dark prevented Patrick from spying on the toys again.

Margaret and Patrick were raised with their 'devoted half-sister'[15] Emily and half-brother James Vincent. Emily was often charged with caring for her siblings and she taught them to read and write. She was patient and encouraging to her eager students and fostered in them a love of reading, which had been nurtured in her by her father. James read widely and his library included books from a variety of genres such as biblical studies, Irish and European history, literary classics and dictionaries. His collection also included a copy of the Koran and biographies of William Cobbett and John Wilkes, both radical journalists and supporters of Catholic emancipation. Although James may have read to his children, it was Emily's magical stories filled with heroic figures and mythical monsters that stimulated their imaginations. In the years that followed, the Pearse children would re-enact many of these early childhood fantasies in the theatrical setting of their parlour.

Margaret and Patrick were constant companions in their formative years, but the arrival of their brother William James (Willie) in 1881 ended forever the close bond they had shared in early childhood. Their mother became seriously ill following Willie's birth and the newborn was sent to be cared for by his grand-uncle Christy and his wife Anne (née Keogh) on their farm in north County Dublin. Willie was reunited with his mother after she had recuperated, but the experience traumatised the entire Pearse family. Patrick later recalled:

> It was a long time before my mother came down to us again. When she did come, looking very pale, one of the first things she did (after pressing my sister and myself to her heart) was to go over and kiss Dobbin; and in gratitude for that gracious kiss I told her that I would consider the little brother (who returned to us the same day) entitled equally with me to bestride that noble steed, as soon as his

little legs should have the necessary length and strength to
grip on. For the present they were obviously too fat for any
such equestrian exercise.[16]

The final addition to the Pearse family arrived in April 1884;
Mary Bridget (later changed to Mary Brigid) was named after her
two grandmothers and her arrival generated much excitement in
the Pearse household. When the nurse announced that the doctor
had brought them a little sister, the children enquired from her
how much their father had paid for the little girl; she replied,
£100. On the day of her birth, their mother placed the infant in
the arms of her siblings.[17]

Less than three months after Mary Brigid's birth, on 5 July
1884, Emily married Alfred Ignatius McGloughlin, an architect
and son of her father's friend John, at St Andrew's Church,
Westland Row. Margaret was a junior bridesmaid at the wedding
and Patrick carried his half-sister's train from the carriage into the
church. Emily described Patrick as 'a comely little page, royally
dressed in ruby velvet and heavy lace, a truly princely little figure;
reserved, shy, and silent, with a wonderfully calm self-possession
which sat strangely on his small figure'.[18]

Margaret, Patrick and Willie enjoyed Emily's wedding, in
particular, the apple pie served at the wedding breakfast. It was not
until the arrival of their beloved Auntie Margaret at the kids' table,
however, that they were completely at ease. Emily's gift to Margaret
and Patrick for carrying out their roles so competently at the
wedding was a scrapbook into which she pasted thousands of
pictures; images of dragons, fairies and giants, as well as red-coated
huntsmen, circus horses, harlequins and clowns. Patrick and
Margaret spent many hours savouring 'a book that was full of
echoes from a world of romantic and far adventure', which was so
large that it took two children to lift.[19] The departure of Emily
from the Pearse home left a void in the life of the children. The
family, however, maintained close ties with Emily and Alfred's
children, Emily Mary (b.1885), Margaret Mary (b.1886) and Alfred

Vincent (b.1888). Indeed, the Pearses were an important support for Emily and her children when Alfred went to New York seeking work and never returned to his family. Left alone, Emily struggled to raise her children and they were placed in an orphanage.[20]

With his second family, James Pearse enjoyed the idyllic home life that had been absent from his first marriage. Margaret was a loving wife and mother with a kind and gentle nature. James was a quiet, mild-mannered man whose deep reserve disappeared when he tenderly embraced each of his children before putting them to bed. James was devoted to his family and took a keen interest in his children's diet and general well-being. In some of the letters written while he was away on business in England, however, he comes across as bossy and occasionally neurotic. He often wrote to his wife instructing her to ensure that she and the children ate nourishing food, were properly attired so they would not catch cold and were cautious around the fire. In one letter, James even reminded his wife to put into a cool place, the succulent beef and ham he had purchased before his departure for England.[21] He encouraged Margaret to bring the children to the seaside on sunny days but cautioned that she should 'be extremely careful with the kiddies' in case they might catch cold.[22] All letters to his wife ended affectionately with kisses for the children: '[k]iss the children dearest for me. Also let them kiss you on my account'[23] and '[t]ell Wow wow and Pat to give you some bigger [kisses] for Papa.'[24]

James's personal happiness coincided with a period of professional success and a foray into the world of political commentary. He kept abreast of political developments in England and was a supporter of the radical Liberal MP, Charles Bradlaugh. James was particularly interested in the agitation for Home Rule and, in 1886, wrote 'A Reply to Professor Maguire's pamphlet "England's duty to Ireland" as it appears to an Englishman' in which he lambasted Maguire's criticism of the Home Rule movement and his offensive anti-nationalist commentary. The publication of this pamphlet, funded entirely by himself, was the culmination of many years of self-education. Recognising the importance of education, James enrolled Margaret and Patrick, aged eight and seven, at a private school run by Mrs Murphy and her daughter at 28 Wentworth Place, Dublin (now Hogan Place), in 1886. They studied a variety of subjects there and were also enrolled in dance classes with Madam Lawton. By all accounts, Patrick did not enjoy the experience and during his time at school labelled Mrs Murphy 'the presiding dragon'.[25]

Within a few months of starting school, the family moved to a new house. The expansion of James's business and family necessitated a move to a larger house and the property on Newbridge Avenue, Sandymount, with its large garden and apple trees, appealed to the young Pearse children, who spent many happy hours there playing with James Vincent and their cousins. However, within a few months of moving to Sandymount, Patrick contracted scarlet fever, an infectious disease that also affected Willie. Their mother's paternal aunt, Margaret, moved in with the family to tend to the sick boys while the girls moved back to Great Brunswick Street, which had not been sold but was rented out to other families, thus providing an additional source of income for the Pearse family.

Auntie Margaret, as she was called by the children, was a strong influence on the young Pearse siblings and the stories she told shaped their imaginations. Although James's father and his older and younger brothers, William and Henry, visited the family in Dublin on a few occasions, the Pearse children had little contact with their father's extended family. In contrast, the children were frequent visitors to their mother's relations and were very familiar with the history of the Brady family. Their colourful ancestors were brought to life by their beloved Auntie Margaret. She regaled the young Pearse children with stories about their great-great-grandfather, Walter Brady, and his family's involvement in the 1798 Rebellion. Walter was a Cavan man who settled in Nobber, County Meath and fought in the Rebellion; his brother was hanged by the Yeomanry and another brother was buried at the

Croppies' Grave at Tara. The family of their great-grandfather, also Walter Brady, were native Irish speakers and steeped in Gaelic culture. Walter had an impressive repertoire of Irish- and English-language songs. He, his wife Margaret (née O'Connor) and eight children, later moved to Dublin to avoid the ravages of famine in north County Meath, but, as a child, his daughter (Auntie Margaret) fondly remembered social gatherings in their home accompanied by music, storytelling and dancing.

The storytelling tradition was perpetuated by Auntie Margaret, who entertained the Pearse children with the legends of Fionn and the Fianna and stories about Robert Emmet, Theobald Wolfe Tone and Napoleon Bonaparte. She sang political ballads about those who died in the 1798 Rebellion and the Fenian Rising of 1867, and the children particularly enjoyed her rendition of 'The Old Grey Mare' (see Appendix 1). Louis Le Roux acknowledged the influence of this elderly grand-aunt who had witnessed the birth of major political and cultural movements in the nineteenth century such as Young Ireland, the Irish Republican Brotherhood, and the Land League. He noted that '[s]he had wept with Ireland, hoped with Ireland and prayed with Ireland for three-quarters of a century.'[26]

Whether she was tending to the Pearse children during illness or just calling to visit, the diminutive figure of Auntie Margaret, her kindly wrinkled face, grey hair tied back in a net and black dress with collar buttoned to the throat, was always welcome.[27] At Sandymount or Great Brunswick Street, they recognised her step on the stairs, ran to greet her, and spent hours creating marvellous stories about the sights and sounds of their neighbourhood. They were fascinated by the doctors making their way to the Children's Hospital, by the sounds of the trams and the mail cars en route to Westland Row, and, in particular, by the man detaching his van from a grey horse and then rewarding the horse's arduous day's work with a feedbag.[28]

The care and love shown by Auntie Margaret to Patrick and Willie during their illness with scarlet fever was later replicated by

Patrick towards his youngest sister. The exact nature of Mary Brigid's illness is unknown, but she suffered ill-health from a young age. She was often confined to bed for extended periods and, consequently, did not receive her education at school. Mary Brigid was often indulged and spoiled as a child. Her social circle consisted of her sister and two brothers, but her closest bond was with Patrick. To say she idolised him would not be an exaggeration. During her periods of convalesence, it was Patrick who temporarily relieved her suffering and boredom by reading about the adventures of fascinating characters in weird and wonderful places. Characters in books, such as *Alice's Adventures in Wonderland*, *Through the Looking-Glass*, *The Merry Adventures of Robin Hood*, *The Wallypug of Why* and *Prince Boohoo and Little Smuts* were brought to life by Patrick, who often sat for hours with his sister. Even at a young age, he was a confident speaker and his dramatic interpretation ensured that stories such as *Uncle Tom's Cabin* became a 'pulsing heart-thrilling reality'.[29] Mary Brigid appreciated the enthusiasm with which he approached every narrative; as she later recalled:

> I was a pitifully delicate child, always ailing and nearly always confined to bed. One of my strongest and pleasantest recollections is that of my brother reading to me every evening when he came home from school. Oh, how I used to yearn for my brother's return! How many times would I ask my mother: 'Are the boys in yet?' How my childish heart would throb tumultuously when at last Pat's quick light step was heard on the stairs, and his eager face appeared in the doorway!

> And then came the long delightful hours of supreme content and quiet rapture, when I could forget my pain and weariness in listening to that tireless fresh young voice. Very often Pat would not even wait to take his dinner, and then mother used to carry *both* dinners up to my room, and

we would eat the meal cosily together, Pat reading and eating at the same time! We used not to speak much, excepting when my brother would explain a word or passage, for both of us were curiously shy. But there was a close bond of sympathy between us, notwithstanding, and we enjoyed our readings immensely.[30]

Mary Brigid and Patrick also enjoyed stories such as 'Doctor Spider' from the *Little Folks* series, or other popular children's stories serialised in *The Strand Magazine,* the Irish weekly, *The Shamrock* and the English Catholic magazine, *St Peter's.* They always delighted in stories about animals and had a fondness for toy animals, Mary Brigid cherishing into adulthood many of the toys Patrick had given her as a child.[31] Mary Brigid spent extended periods on her own, so gifts such as a swan made from celluloid and a family of pigs fashioned from a pen-wiper helped her to pass 'away many a weary hour of loneliness and pain'.[32] Patrick wrote a weekly newspaper for the family that included short articles, jokes, puzzles, and a regular story entitled 'Pat Murphy's Pig'. Although the weekly newspaper was handwritten in an ordinary exercise book, Mary Brigid keenly awaited its weekly arrival. In fact, she delighted in any opportunity to spend time with her brother.

One could argue that the remarkable respect for and insight into children's minds which Patrick displayed in the latter part of his life was formed during the time he spent educating his younger sister and fostering in her a love of learning. The hours that Patrick and Mary Brigid spent together as children definitely had a lasting effect on both siblings. Mary Brigid wrote plays, children's stories and a novel. Patrick was inspired by Mary Brigid's childhood convalesence to write several children's stories that included sick children as characters such as 'An Gadaí' and 'Eoghainín na nÉan'. In 'Eoghainín na nÉan', Patrick told the poignant story of a terminally ill young boy called Eoghainín, who longs for the arrival of the swallows. When they finally arrive, he spends hours listening to tales of their adventures in other countries. As the time approaches for them to migrate to warmer climes, Eoghainín tells his mother that he will depart with them; they watch the swallows leave and, as the last pair fly off, Eoghainín rests his head on his mother's shoulder and dies. As children, Mary Brigid and Patrick loved to watch the arrival of migratory birds and, in later life, the comings and goings of the swallows always reminded Mary Brigid of her brother.

In between periods of convalescence, Mary Brigid participated fully in the family's escapades. The young Pearses had a particular fondness for all things theatrical and loved to dress up and to disguise themselves as different characters. Clothes were borrowed from their mother's rag-bag, or sometimes her wardrobe and Patrick was never rebuked by his mother for taking her seal coat or best silk dress to be used as costumes for the performances.[33] Patrick was often joined by his cousin Mary Kate Kelly or his nephew Alfred McGloughlin to play pranks on unsuspecting neighbours or passers by. Alfred recounted the story of when he and Patrick dressed as beggars for a day, travelling around Donnybrook. Alfred came away with nothing but Patrick received a donation of several shillings from a generous elderly lady.[34] On another occasion, Patrick and Willie dressed in old clothes and sold apples to help poor children in the neighbourhood. Unfortunately, their charitable endeavours were soon stymied when a group of local 'ragged boys', who resented the Pearse brothers appropriating their business, beat them up. Mary Brigid described the encounter in detail noting that, although the brothers tried to defend themselves, they were outnumbered and were relieved when a teenage neighbour intervened to rescue them.[35]

The Pearse siblings, together with their cousins, nieces and nephews, transformed their drawing room into a stage and performed adaptations of Shakespearean plays or short plays written by Patrick. Each of the children embraced their various roles with enthusiasm. In a performance of *Macbeth*, with Patrick in the title role and Mary Brigid playing Lady Macbeth, Mary Brigid remembered how Patrick did not always approach his roles in a serious, professional manner:

> Unfortunately, however, Pat's risibility always completely overcame him the instant he addressed me by any endearing term, and he used to break into uncontrollable laughter! This made the whole business absolutely farcical. To see the grave Scotsman holding his sides with hilarity, to hear his helpless peals of mirth was too ridiculous. I used to become seriously annoyed. I would work up the scene most dramatically, and then Pat would ruin it.[36]

Patrick wrote his first play, *The Rival Lovers*, at the age of nine and cast Mary Brigid, then only five years old, in a lead role. Patrick and Willie assumed the lead male roles and Mary Kate played Mary Brigid's mother. During the dramatic duel scene, Mary Brigid was caught in the crossfire and dramatically fell to her death as directed by Patrick. In the years that followed, Patrick wrote several plays for his siblings and relations, including *The Pride of Finisterre* and *Brian Boru*. *The Pride of Finisterre*, set in the Spanish countryside, was an ambitious production written in verse form for eight characters. Mary Brigid played the role of Eugénie (the 'Pride of Finisterre'), Willie played her lover, Bernard, Margaret was cast in the role of a noblewoman called Marie d'Artua, and Patrick played her villainous husband, Count Alexander.

Lesser roles were allocated to their cousin Mary Kate, who played Eugénie's mother, and her brother, John, who acted as a priest. Patrick also adapted some scenes from *Uncle Tom's Cabin* for performance and wrote a play about love and jealousy that Mary Brigid set to music and performed as a mini opera. The young thespians savoured these early performances and the response of their audiences. As Mary Brigid later wrote, 'I don't believe that *any* of the greatest actors on the stage ever felt such exquisite delight when they received the plaudits of a vast audience as *we* felt when we "took our curtain" amidst wild clapping from our friends! It was simply the perfection of joy!'[37]

The subject matter of their performances was not limited to great works of literature or Patrick's compositions. The young theatrical troupe often acted out religious ceremonies that they had attended at their local church in Westland Row. This church played an important role in the religious upbringing of the Pearse children. Each of them was baptised, received their First Confession, First Holy Communion and Confirmation in this church, and Margaret and Patrick later taught classes in catechism there on Sundays. Margaret recalled that, even in his youth, Patrick had a talent for delivering impressive lectures, especially on religious subjects. At the age of nine, he delivered an insightful sermon to his family on the transfiguration of Jesus Christ; Margaret later wondered how a boy of his age had acquired such a grasp and appreciation of Christian doctrine.[38] In their re-enactments of religious ceremonies, Patrick regularly played the role of boy-priest, Willie acted as his acolyte, and the others were his devoted congregation. Unfortunately, the solemnity of the occasion was often interrupted by bickering between Margaret and her younger siblings. Mary Brigid claimed that she and Willie disliked Margaret's domineering manner, and Patrick was often forced to act as peacemaker 'for his grave reasonableness was very forceful'.[39]

Despite his apparent piety, it seems Patrick was the most mischievous of the Pearse children and had a tendency to laugh uncontrollably at the most inappropriate moments. When a fire broke out in Margaret's room, Patrick quickly grabbed her bedclothes and a rug to quench the flames. After his heroic deeds, Patrick was overcome by a fit of giggles. Margaret, however, was not amused to find that her cherished bed linen and furniture had been destroyed by a cackling firefighter. Mary Brigid wondered whether 'Pat's loud laughter in the midst of smoke and fire, or Maggie's woe-begone face as she surveyed her bedraggled apartment afterwards' was the more ridiculous.[40]

Patrick's love of sweet things was also a cause of contention in the Pearse household. When a pane of glass became loose in the landing window of their home, their father affixed some sticky gelatine sweets to prevent the pane from falling out. Later that evening, James noticed that his temporary confectionary glue was slowly disappearing and soon discovered that his eldest son could not resist taking a sweet every time he passed by the window.[41] Similarly, whenever their mother left a freshly-baked rich cake with nut topping on the kitchen table, Patrick would invariably consume the nutty topping and leave the remainder of the uneaten cake behind.[42]

One Christmas, their mother enlisted the help of her children to make a Christmas cake and pudding. To expedite the process, Mary Brigid chopped the suet, Margaret crumbled and grated the bread, Willie beat the eggs, and Patrick stoned the raisins. Unfortunately, Patrick's love of sweets, nuts, sugar barley and Turkish delight meant that he consumed more fruit than he stoned. Their mother eventually discovered the considerable reduction in the amount of fruit. She did not chastise her eldest son but moved him to another job, slicing the candied peel. Patrick, however, could not resist the temptation of the sweet candied peel and was eventually relieved of his duties. Following his dismissal, he stretched out on the sofa in the front room and started singing, but he was quickly ordered out of the room by his father who could not bear the racket.

Mary Brigid later filled the pages of her book, *The Home-Life of Pádraig Pearse* (1934), with similar stories about their childhood antics and, invariably, cast Patrick as the central protagonist, 'Pat was the leading incentive and presiding spirit of our small company.'[43] She related an incident when the Pearses visited their half-sister Emily's house. The children were happily playing tennis and other games in a field behind the house until they were ordered out by the landlord. Their niece Emily explained to the landlord that he had agreed to let them play in the field and Patrick cheekily retorted, 'then we *will* play!' and so they did.[44]

As the Pearse children grew older, Patrick and Margaret focused increasingly on their education and achieving excellence in their studies, thus allowing less time to partake in the fun they enjoyed as young children. Memories of their idyllic childhood remained with them throughout their lives. In adult life, Patrick wrote in his autobiography of his desire to return to the serenity of his childhood and 'to be at home always, with the same beloved faces, the same familiar shapes and sounds'.[45] They squabbled, as all siblings do, but James and Margaret ensured that their children grew up in a stable, close-knit and loving family; a happy home where the children's creative talents flourished.

CHAPTER 2

From Girlhood to Womanhood

I have never loved any place better than those old places; or any voice better than those old voices. I have been faithful to them in my heart even when I have deliberately turned my feet from them, seeking far places and far voices.[1]

Patrick Pearse

Eighteen ninety-one was a significant year in the education of the Pearse family as three of the four children, Margaret, Patrick and Willie, started secondary school. Patrick and Willie were enrolled at the Christian Brothers School (CBS) in Westland Row and Margaret, aged thirteen, commenced her studies at the Sisters of the Holy Faith School, Clarendon Street, which opened in 1873. Margaret excelled at school, receiving first place in all subjects. She had a particular talent for public speaking, and French, music and embroidery were her favourite classes. Margaret praised the school's monthly system of oral examinations in all subjects which created a competitive environment among the students. She was diligent and often studied through the night for the monthly examinations set by visiting sisters from the Holy Faith convent in Glasnevin. Margaret's exceptional memory ensured that she could easily memorise lengthy texts and data. She enjoyed being challenged intellectually and eagerly anticipated the weekly visits of the Vincentian priest Fr John Gowan (co-founder of the Sisters of the Holy Faith order) who invariably posed difficult linguistic and mathematical questions.

On one occasion, he recited the numbers one to ten in Latin. In preparation for his next visit, Margaret, the school's most exemplary student, was asked by the Headmistress to memorise as many English derivatives of the ten Latin numerals as she could. Margaret succeeded in memorising seventy derivatives which greatly impressed Fr Gowan.[2] Another frequent visitor to the school was Fr Murphy, a curate at Westland Row Church, who encouraged the girls to improve their public speaking. Margaret was presented with several prizes by him for her recitation of poetry; her favourite prize was a needlework set which she treasured forever.[3]

Throughout her life, Margaret spoke in glowing terms of her alma mater and of teachers including Sr Mary Winifred, the Headmistress, Sr Mary Juliana, who taught French, and Sr Mary Joseph, who taught a variety of subjects. As many of her teachers were in their early twenties, Margaret proudly observed that 'we were [all] young together.'[4] In the *Centenary Magazine of the Holy Faith Sisters* of 1967, she reminisced about the school's annual Prize Distribution Day where students showcased their talents in recitation and the performance of instrumental and vocal music. In the article, she recalled two poems, *Ave Maria* and *The Uninvited Guest* (known as *St Gregory's Guest*) by John Greenleaf Whittier, which she had recited at the school's Distribution Day almost seventy-five years previously. She described it as '[o]ne of the happiest days in Clarendon Street'.[5] When the Holy Faith Past Pupils' Union was established in 1933, Margaret became president of the Clarendon branch and was honoured to be elected honorary life president of the Past Pupils' Union.[6]

The Pearse home was a religious one, but Margaret's strong religious faith was also nurtured at school and through membership of the Sodality of the Holy Angels. On Tuesdays, she attended recitations of the Litany of the Angels and, on Saturdays, she participated in the Sodality of the Holy Angels. Many of these religious practices she acquired as a child were continued in adulthood. After completing her studies at the Holy Faith School, she studied for a qualification in domestic economy at the Rathmines Technical Institute (College of Commerce) and, in 1907, she received a certificate of competency from the Leinster College of Irish.

Patrick and Willie's experience of secondary education at the CBS would have been similar to Margaret's. The Christian Brothers' approach, which promoted rote learning and exam-focused curricula, suited Patrick and he passed four grades of the Intermediate examination between 1893 and 1896. A system of rote memorisation did not appeal to Willie and he struggled academically in his years at the CBS. He sat a preparatory examination in 1895, but failed all subjects except Irish. In 1897, aged fifteen, Willie enrolled in evening classes at the Metropolitan School of Art in Kildare Street, Dublin. He enrolled initially as a part-time student, as he was also working during the day as an apprentice sculptor at the family business alongside his father and half-brother, James Vincent, who was a stone carver. He remained registered as a student, some years as a part-time student, but occasionally in full-time study, for the next fifteen years.[7] Willie later attended art courses in Paris and at the Royal College of Art in London.

Due to her illness, it is unlikely that Mary Brigid received a formal education like her siblings. She did not attend Mrs Murphy's School and is not listed as a student of the Holy Faith School. Although she was briefly enrolled at the Metropolitan School of Art with Willie and took a course in German at the Rathmines College of Commerce in 1915, it seems likely that she was primarily educated at home.[8] As her older siblings became increasingly occupied with their studies and school commitments, Mary Brigid spent much of the day on her own. Patrick's schoolwork, in particular, claimed most of his attention and, consequently, he could not spend time with Mary Brigid reading to her or teaching her the Irish language. She fondly remembered the time they spent together in childhood, but was conscious that he was no longer a child and lamented his transition to adulthood:

> Although my brother always retained his boyishness, he *grew up* sooner than any of us! I well remember how surprised I was – and rather contemptuous, I fear – when I first heard him call 'mother' instead of 'mama', as we all used to do before! Afterwards came a queer feeling of *blankness* as I began to realise that Pat was rapidly becoming – a *man*![9]

Mary Brigid showed considerable aptitude for music from a young age and was recognised as the most musically talented of the Pearse family. As a young girl, Patrick asked her to set one of his poems, entitled 'Mother', to music. When Mary Brigid later performed her arrangement of the song for her own mother, 'tears of pride and joy came into her eyes as she listened, gazing proudly and fondly upon her "boy"'.[10] Mary Brigid, Patrick and Margaret received piano lessons; Patrick, however, did not progress past simple arrangements of 'Vesper Hymn' and 'Nelly Bly'. It seems that, although Patrick maintained an interest in music all his life and attended performances of operas by the German composer Richard Wagner in Dublin, he had little aptitude for music. Mary Brigid noted that, despite her best efforts to teach him, he never mastered the art of singing:

> I used to try him with the scale sometimes, and the result was always excruciatingly funny! He would start off with a most tremendous seriousness and intone in rather a wavering manner: 'Doh!' More quaveringly still, and very much out of tune, would come 'Ray!' Then, with an appalling suddenness, he would go completely off the scale, and his 'Me!' would be at least five notes too high![11]

Unlike Patrick, Mary Brigid went on to become an accomplished pianist and later studied theory and harmony with Carl Hardebeck, a noted organist, folk-song collector and leading figure in the Gaelic League and Feis Ceoil. Hardebeck was famed for his arrangements of Irish folk songs, and his style influenced Mary Brigid's arrangements of Irish airs for voice and harp, and voice and piano, many of which are kept at the Pearse Archive in Kilmainham Gaol.

As the Pearse children grew and developed, it became increasingly clear that Patrick was the force that united them. Ruth Dudley Edwards described the children as a 'mixed bunch' in which '[a]ll the will seems to have gone into the two eldest, Margaret and Patrick, while the young pair, Willie and Mary Bridget [sic] … were natural followers'.[12] Mary Brigid and Willie may have been 'natural followers', but they were undoubtedly enthusiastic ones, as Patrick took a genuine interest in each of his siblings' pursuits. Much has been written about the close bond that existed between Patrick and Willie. They attended the same school, socialised together and enjoyed pastimes such as boxing. Each of the sisters also shared interests with Patrick. Margaret and Patrick's close bond was centred around their shared passions of religion and education. They regularly attended religious services together, such as the ceremonies of Holy Week and Forty Hours' Devotion at St Andrew's Church, Westland Row. Patrick and Margaret made annual visits on the 2nd of August to the Church of the Immaculate Conception, Merchant's Quay to gain a plenary indulgence from the Portiuncula Indulgence or the Pardon Prayer of St Francis.

On one occasion, Patrick was so keen to gain an indulgence that he jumped off a moving tram after it failed to stop near the church. Unfortunately, he was injured and his face was covered in blood. Fearing that he might be stopped and questioned by police, Patrick ran home.[13] Their attendance at religious ceremonies was, however, usually less dramatic. Mary Brigid and Patrick shared a love of the Irish language and Irish folklore. He fostered in her a love of the language by teaching her to read and write Gaelic script, which he had been taught at the CBS. Patrick also read aloud passages from books he studied on Irish legends, including tales about Diarmuid and Gráinne and the death of Cúchulainn.[14]

Each of the siblings in turn devoted themselves to whichever project Patrick was most passionate about at the time. After he completed his studies, he was appointed pupil-teacher at Westland Row. Too young to enter university, he occupied his time with the development and promotion of Irish culture and the Irish language. In 1896, he and his friend and classmate Edward (Éamonn) O'Neill formed the New Ireland Literary Society. The first of the Society's regular weekly meetings took place on 1 December 1896 at the Star and Garter Hotel in D'Olier Street. This debating and literary society was an important forum for Patrick to showcase his talents and to hone his skills as an orator. He delivered lectures, participated in debates, gave recitations, and contributed to the Society's journal, *Debate*. Topics embraced a wide range of subjects. On 19 January 1897, the debate was 'That Ireland is Becoming Anglicised'[15] and on 1 March 1898, Edward O'Neill, E.A. Murray and James Creevey debated the motion 'That Rudyard Kipling is not a true poet'.[16]

Irish themes, however, generally dominated the debates. Although Willie participated in a debate in February 1898 on the motion 'That the Milesian Invasion of Ireland as Recorded by the Bards is a Myth', Patrick was the central and most active member of the Society,[17] giving three lectures on Irish subjects between March 1897 and January 1898, including his inaugural presidential address, 'The Intellectual Future of the Gael', on 19 October 1897 at Costigan's Hotel, Upper O'Connell Street.[18] This lecture along with 'Gaelic Prose Literature' and 'The Folk Songs of Ireland' were published as *Three Lectures on Gaelic Topics* by M.H. Gill & Son in 1898.

Mary Brigid and Margaret performed at several of the Society's social evenings. In April 1897, the sisters performed a piano duet, *Whispers from Erin* (*c*.1860) by William Smyth

Rockstro. This fantasy for piano was based on two popular contemporary Irish airs, 'Oft in the Stilly Night' and 'The Young May Moon' by Thomas Moore. Mary Brigid also played an arrangement of the overture to the *Lily of Killarney* (1862) by Julius Benedict and was listed as the accompanist for the evening, despite being only thirteen years of age.[19] The evening also included recitations by Patrick and Edward O'Neill from William Shakespeare's *Julius Caesar* and *Hamlet*. Despite the small stage and lack of costumes or backdrop, the recitations were entertaining and well received; the performances of various amateur singers, however, were less impressive.

Mary Brigid was tasked with accompanying the singers, none of whom provided sheet music for accompaniment. When she asked Patrick if he had any idea what key might best suit their voices, he replied the 'common or garden key'.[20] She informed him that there was no such key, but he reassured her that they all sang in a standard key. Baffled by his ignorance, she left him 'blissfully unconscious of his absurdity'.[21] Mary Brigid's considerable musical ability and acute musical ear enabled her to accompany the various performers on the night by vamping along with chords. Towards the end of the evening, however, one of the soloists who impressed her with his excellent voice during rehearsal, struggled to sing in tune. She later recalled the horrific experience:

> he had a nice voice. Afterwards his song would also have been very nice if he had only remained in the one key, instead of roaming through about six! For three verses of 'The Risin' of the Moon' I chased him madly all over the piano, wondering which of us would break down first. By the time the moon had fully risen the piano part was ended, and I was a complete wreck! Pat's 'common or garden key' seemed to have rather an elastic compass![22]

The New Ireland Literary Society disbanded in 1898 because Patrick was increasingly preoccupied with his studies and his

involvement in the Gaelic League (Conradh na Gaeilge), founded
in 1893 by Douglas Hyde and Eoin MacNeill to preserve Irish as
the national language of Ireland and to encourage the study of
Gaelic literature. In 1887, the Society for the Preservation of the
Irish Language had also attempted to promote Irish by advocating
that it should be taught in schools and spoken more frequently,
but it was the League that would succeed in popularising the
language and reviving various Gaelic practices. The final decades
of the nineteenth century were marked by the formation of
various cultural movements, such as the Gaelic Athletic Association
(1884), the National Literary Society (1892), Feis Ceoil (1896)
and the Irish Literary Theatre (1898). These movements were part
of the reawakening of a national Irish consciousness and a renewal
of national spirit, which it was hoped would result in increased
cultural and material prosperity.

The Pearse siblings participated in many contemporary
cultural movements. They were, undoubtedly, influenced by
Patrick's cultural interests, which primarily centred around the
promotion and development of the Irish language. The family's
participation in cultural movements was not unusual as many
young people were involved in cultural and/or political activism
during this period. As Mary Colum, the author and literary critic
commented, young people had 'a desire for self-sacrifice, a
devotion to causes; everyone was working for a cause, for
practically everything was a cause'.[23]

Patrick was the first of the Pearse family to join the Gaelic
League, in 1896, and was soon followed by Willie and Mary
Brigid. From 1897 onwards, he became more prominent in the
League and more vocal at branch meetings. He was an active
contributor to the weekly bilingual newspaper *Fáinne an Lae*, and,
in 1898, was co-opted on to the Executive Committee (Coiste
Gnótha). In the spring of 1898, he sat the Matriculation and
shortly after commenced studying for a Bachelor of Arts in
French, English and Celtic (Irish) at the Royal University, and a
Bachelor of Law at the King's Inns and Trinity College, Dublin.

Patrick's participation in the activities of the Gaelic League often distracted him from his studies, but his commitment to the organisation resulted in his appointment as secretary of the Publications Committee from 1900 to 1903 and editor of its newspaper, *An Claidheamh Soluis* (The Sword of Light), in 1903.

The burden of work often took its toll on Patrick but his family were at hand to support him, even to the point of ensuring that he was not late for giving lectures or attending Sunday morning mass. When the Pearse family lived in Sandymount, each of them took it in turn to call Patrick from 8.00am onwards for midday mass at St Andrew's Church. Despite never leaving the house before 11.53am, when the train signals dropped, he never missed the train.[24] Patrick's tardiness, and apparently, chaotic life, intrigued his younger sister who wrote a humorous account of several memorable incidents.

> As the shrill whistle sounded, and the train steamed into the station, he would be seen sprinting up the platform, triumphant and breathless. Once or twice he just hung on, and was hauled into the guard's van. The porters all got to know the eccentric gentleman who was always late, and would courteously keep a door open, and push his flying figure into the carriage in the nick of time.[25]

She recalled sitting in lecture theatres waiting for Patrick to deliver a lecture knowing that he would probably arrive thirty minutes late for the lecture as he was invariably fast asleep on the couch in the drawing room of their home.

Willie's association with the Gaelic League began in 1898. He spoke the language fluently and, in between studying, participating in student exhibitions and working, also taught an Irish language class at the Metropolitan School of Art. Mary Brigid's connection with the League was through Patrick and her harp teacher, Owen Lloyd. Mary Brigid's fascination with the harp began after she attended a concert featuring a pedal harpist at the Round Room of the Rotunda in Dublin. She expressed an interest in acquiring a harp, but following the closure of Francis Hewson's Irish and pedal harp manufactory in York Street, Dublin, in 1872, it became increasingly difficult to source an instrument in Ireland. Nevertheless, knowing how enthusiastic she was about the instrument, Patrick eventually purchased a harp for her.

The memory of getting her first harp remained with Mary Brigid for the rest of her life: 'I still remember the intense rapture with which I at last held the long-wished-for treasure in my trembling arms. I just *loved* my harp; and I am proud to say that, despite many vicissitudes, the same precious little instrument can sing to-day as sweetly as it sang in those far-off happy days so long gone by!'[26] Ruth Dudley Edwards described Patrick's generosity as 'a symptom of his engaging open-handedness and disregard for economic pressures';[27] perhaps it was merely Patrick fostering his sister's talents again as he had done so often during her childhood.

It is most likely that Mary Brigid was introduced to Owen Lloyd by Patrick. Lloyd was a renowned Irish, pedal and wire-strung harpist and Irish language activist, who, through his busy performing career and teaching duties, transformed the perception and repertoire of the Irish harp in the late nineteenth and early twentieth centuries.[28] The tradition of wire-strung Irish harp performance had been in decline for centuries, but inspired by the ideologies of various cultural movements of the late nineteenth century, Lloyd was determined to revive an interest in the performance and teaching of the modern Irish harp in Ireland and amongst the Irish disapora in England and Scotland. Both Patrick and Lloyd were prominent members of the Gaelic League and attended several League events together, including the Mayo Feis in April 1903, at which Lloyd performed to great acclaim. Under Lloyd's guidance, Mary Brigid progressed quickly on the Irish and concert harps.

Lloyd was a member of the committees of An tOireachtas, a major competitive festival organised by the Gaelic League, and Feis Ceoil, an association that promoted Irish music through concerts and annual competitions. Lloyd's membership of these committees afforded opportunities for his most promising students to perform. Before 1898, branch meetings of the Gaelic League comprised a language class followed by a discussion or debate. The League made little progress in attracting new membership in its early years, having only forty-three branches in 1897. In November 1897, Patrick proposed at a branch meeting that weekly meetings could be made more appealing through a series of lectures and concerts under the auspices of the League. He also suggested that music, drama or dancing be used to attract new members. Gradually, the League restructured and branches (*craobhacha*) at regional and local level added musical performances, and lectures on Irish history, folklore and culture, to their existing language classes. Branch meetings, particularly in Dublin, began to conform to a practice of concluding with a performance of songs in Irish or with a short recital on the uilleann pipes or harp; Mary Brigid performed regularly at these branch meetings.

In early 1900, Mary Brigid played at monthly meetings of the central branch in Dublin; many of these meetings were chaired by her brother Patrick. Committee members from the branch organised a *scoraíocht* (social evening), on 10 January, which featured Thomas Rowsome on pipes, pianists, dancers and singers. Mary Brigid performed a selection of harp pieces and sang 'Bán Chnoic Éireann Ó' to an enthusiastic audience of over a hundred people.[29] The following month, at another branch meeting, she gave a short recital on the harp which included Thomas Moore's 'Has Sorrow Thy Young Days Shaded' and 'Garryowen with Variations'.[30] Her repertoire, which included old harp tunes, song airs and early nineteenth-century compositions by Moore, reflected the varied nature of music performed on Irish harps in this period.

Feiseanna (competitions), both regional and national, and *aeríochtaí* (concerts) were also an important means of attracting new membership to the League and were crucial media for the revival of various Gaelic practices, such as dancing, piping and

Irish harp performance. Eighteen ninety-seven marked the inauguration of An tOireachtas, a new competition under the auspices of the Gaelic League. Lloyd performed regularly at concerts of An tOireachtas and was joined in 1898 by his band of harps, an ensemble consisting of three or four of his harp students who performed two-part arrangements of a repertoire including 'Carolan's Concerto', 'Dear Harp of my Country' and 'Return from Fingal'.[31] In May 1900, Mary Brigid, Miss Butler, Nora Twemlow, Nora Collins and Lloyd played 'Siúd Síos fa mo Dhídean' and 'An Filleadh ó Fhine Ghall'. The band of harps was a regular feature at concerts of An tOireachtas during the first decade of its existence.[32]

Mary Brigid also won several prizes at harp competitions run by An tOireachtas. To acknowledge her success, Patrick purchased a second Irish harp for her, made by James McFall of 22 York Lane, Belfast. The McFall harp, which was strung with gut, was the most advanced contemporary Irish harp. It could be played in thirteen different keys, had a rich tone, and was beautifully decorated in old Celtic ornamentation. Mary Brigid later used this harp to teach students at St Enda's School, Rathfarnham; this instrument now forms part of the exhibit at the Pearse Museum.[33]

By the end of the nineteenth century, Margaret, Patrick, Willie and Mary Brigid were enjoying active lives as members of, and contributors to, various cultural movements in Dublin. Their carefree lifestyles were facilitated by the success of Pearse and Sons Monumental Sculptors. In the final decade of the nineteenth century, James had secured prestigious commissions for altars, fonts, carvings, monuments, tablets, and all kinds of marble, stone and granite works. His work could be seen in churches all over Ireland from John's Lane Church and the mortuary chapel, Glasnevin Cemetery, in Dublin, to the Church of the Immaculate Conception in Strabane and St Saviour's Church in Waterford. The Pearse family's idyllic home life, however, was shattered by James's sudden death on 5 September 1900. He died from a cerebral haemorrhage while visiting his brother in Birmingham.

His body was brought back to his home in George's Villa, Sandymount where he was waked, and his requiem mass was concelebrated at Westland Row Church by Fr Galvin and Fr Murphy, the Administrator.[34] His death marked a new phase in the lives of Margaret, Patrick, Willie, Mary Brigid and their mother.

CHAPTER 3

A Pearse Family Project

What would you think if later on I were to take all these
things and in a bigger house start a school of my own?[1]

Patrick Pearse

At the time of James Pearse's death, the family were living at
5 George's Villa, Sandymount. Over the next few years, they
moved frequently, initially to 363 Sandymount Avenue and later
to 'Liosán' Lisreaghan Terrace, Sandymount, and 39 Marlborough
Road, Donnybrook. During this period, various relations lived
with them, including their cousins, Mary Kate and John Kelly
who were orphaned after the deaths of their parents, John and
Catherine (Margaret Pearse's sister). John junior's untimely death
at the age of sixteen years on 14 November 1902 from injuries
sustained after he was knocked off his bicycle by a bread van
shocked the family. His death, coupled with the loss of their
father, James, their mother's sister Catherine (d.1887), their
maternal grandmother (d.1888) and grandfather (d.1894), and
their beloved auntie Margaret (d.1892) deeply affected the Pearse
family, in particular, Mary Brigid, who struggled to come to
terms with the loss of anyone from her close-knit circle of family
and friends. However, the strain of running the family business
absorbed much of their time and energy and provided a temporary
distraction from their grief.

James Pearse died intestate, leaving an estate valued at
£1,470.17s.6d. Pearse and Sons was then a thriving business with
premises at 27 Great Brunswick Street, and a number of properties
on Townsend Street. After her husband's death, Mrs Pearse helped
in the running of the business, together with James Vincent and
Willie. Patrick also worked at the family business in between
periods training as a barrister at the King's Inns. Patrick was called
to the Bar in 1901 but, apart from representing the Gaelic League
in a case against the Post Office in 1905 for its refusal to deliver
post addressed in the Irish language, he did not pursue a legal
career.

Nineteen hundred and five was to prove a significant year for
Patrick and his family. In addition to being appointed secretary to
the Gaelic League, on the 22nd of June he also embarked on a
four-week trip to Belgium with his sister Margaret to observe
methods of teaching languages and approaches to bilingualism at
some thirty institutions. Patrick was critical of the Irish education
system under British administration and, for many years, both he
and Margaret shared an interest in reforming it. He condemned
teaching methodologies and rejected rote learning, the payment
by results system, exam-orientated curricula and corporal
punishment. Patrick's early educational philosophy outlined in
An Claidheamh Soluis was influenced by the pedagogical theories
on child-centred education espoused by Johann Heinrich
Pestalozzi and his student, Friedrich Froebel. He was also inspired
by the writings of prominent Gaelic Leaguers, such as Eoin
MacNeill, Douglas Hyde and Michael O'Hickey. Patrick believed
that the regeneration of Ireland would be achieved through
educating her youth; consequently, he set about researching how
modern European pedagogical methods could be incorporated
into the Irish education system. His objective was essentially to
achieve 'educational home rule' for Ireland.[2]

On their trip to Belgium, Patrick and Margaret experienced
first-hand how bilingual teaching was practised in over twenty
State primary and secondary schools, a number of infant schools,

two voluntary schools, including the Jesuit School de Saint Michel in Brussels, one industrial school and two universities. Patrick identified three main objectives of the Belgian bilingual system of teaching, namely, 'that every Belgian child is entitled first and foremost to be taught his mother-tongue; that every Belgian child is entitled to be taught, in addition, one of the other languages spoken in Belgium; and that all language teaching ought to be on the "direct method"'.[3] In a number of the schools, Patrick delivered short lectures about Ireland to the students; he told the students that 'the Irish, like the Flemings, were making a great stand for their language'.[4]

Though the school visits were supported by the Belgian Ministry of Public Instruction, the trip lasted longer than he had anticipated because of difficulties in obtaining permission to visit certain schools. Although Margaret and Patrick went together to École Froebel, an infant school in Antwerp, she did not accompany him on his trips to schools in Brussels, Laeken, Malines, Ghent and Bruges. Nevertheless, Margaret enjoyed the trip as it was an opportunity to spend time with her brother. It also proved to be an edifyingly cultural experience despite the fact that the siblings' attitudes to Belgian culture differed greatly.

Coming from an artistic family, they delighted in Belgium's numerous art galleries, though Margaret's appetite for such cultural activities did not match that of her brother and she often sat down while Patrick continued alone on his tour. Margaret noted that '[t]he pictures appealed to the artist in him [Patrick]; the people to his wonderful sympathy with human nature – its virtues and failings, its griefs and joys!'[5] The buildings and monuments dedicated to Belgium's freedom also appealed to Patrick. Standing in front of the Belgian Houses of Parliament, Margaret recalled her brother's observation on the suitability of the term *Le Palais de la Nation* (Palace of the Nation) to describe their national parliament. He was impressed by the beauty of the Belgian countryside and enjoyed meeting people of different nationalities. One Sunday morning after visiting various churches in Antwerp, he suggested going to a Chinese restaurant for a meal. Margaret did not share her brother's enthusiasm for foreign cuisine and persuaded him to leave the restaurant before their orders were taken. During their trip, Patrick purchased three *objets d'art* for Margaret. Their purchases, however, were kept to a minimum as Patrick discouraged Margaret from unnecessarily spending too much money outside Ireland.

Their homeland was never far from their thoughts. Patrick did not like being away from home and the extended trip also caused anxiety for him in his role as editor of *An Claidheamh Soluis*. As they arrived back in Dublin, Patrick proudly remarked that their native city could compete with any of the places they had seen on their travels. The trip to Belgium had a profound effect on his pedagogical theories and he published a series of articles entitled 'Belgium and its Schools' in *An Claidheamh Soluis* from August 1905 to March 1907 aimed at primary and secondary school teachers, Gaelic League teachers, educationalists and language activists generally.

Margaret put some of her pedagogical theories into practice. In 1907, she established a small preparatory school for girls and boys at their home near Leeson Park, Donnybrook. The school was modelled on Mrs Murphy's school, the first school that she, Patrick and Willie attended. The drawing room of the house was used for school lessons, the dining room was transformed into a ballroom for dance classes, and the spacious garden provided the children with a suitable playground. Margaret's brothers supported her in this endeavour and occasionally taught at the school. Patrick also ensured that the aesthetics of the classroom were conducive to a positive learning environment. The day before the school opened, he purchased wall charts to enhance the classroom space. Patrick confided in Margaret his desire to emulate her success by establishing his own school, saying '[w]hat would you think if later on I were to take all these things and in a bigger house start a school of my own?'[6] To realise those aspirations, Patrick needed the complete support of his entire family;

consequently, Margaret's preparatory school was soon incorporated into his own educational project.

On 8 September 1908, Patrick opened St Enda's College/Scoil Éanna, the first bilingual, lay Catholic school for boys (day and boarding) at Cullenswood House, Oakley Road, Ranelagh, Dublin. The house, an old Georgian property, was the birthplace of the historian and MP, William Lecky. St Enda's, which was the culmination of many years of Patrick's research into education systems and methodologies, marked the beginning of an educational journey that consumed the lives of the entire Pearse family. The motto of the school was 'truth on our lips, strength in our hands and purity in our hearts'. The project was pioneering in its promotion of child-centred education, creativity and personal development, and liberal teaching methods. The objective of the school was to produce well-rounded students educated in a distinctly Irish setting. Consequently, instead of placing emphasis on the memorisation of information to achieve excellent examination results, Pearse endeavoured to develop the unique character of each of his students. He modelled his ideology on an early Irish system which focused on the relationship between the fosterer and the foster-child.

Every aspect of the educational experience was considered, from the interior décor and colour scheme to the furnishings and art works in each classroom. Patrick employed some of the leading Irish artists and artisans to renovate and decorate Cullenswood House. The interior of the school was adorned with original paintings by Æ (George Russell) and Jack B. Yeats, and sculptures and friezes by Willie. The artwork was chosen to cultivate a love of art and an appreciation of the students' surroundings. Beatrice Elvery's painting *Íosagán* was displayed in the school's main classroom and Sarah Purser designed a stained-glass panel for the front door of the house. A carved panel of Cúchulainn by Edwin Morrow with the much-quoted phrase from *Táin Bó Cúailnge*, 'I care not though I were to live but one day and one night provided my fame and my deeds live after me', was intended to inspire the students. These interior visual elements, the building itself and its grounds were integral to Patrick's vision of educational excellence.

Patrick assumed the role of headmaster; Thomas MacDonagh was assistant headmaster; Tomás MacDomhnaill (Thomas MacDonnell) taught athletics, dancing and music; Fr W. Landers was appointed school chaplain and Willie taught art classes. Part-time teachers were also employed. These included Michael Smithwick (higher mathematics and mathematical science); Dr Patrick Doody (classics); Thomas O'Nolan (ancient classics); John P. Henry (Irish); Vincent O'Brien (piano and voice); Owen Lloyd (violin and harp); Joseph Clarke (manual instruction); John A. Clinch (commercial subjects); and William Carroll (gymnastics and drill). Staff and students of the school produced two magazines, *An Scoláire* (*The Scholar*) and *An Macaomh* (*The Youth*) (1909–13).

Forty boys were enrolled at the school in its first year. They were offered a wide-ranging curriculum including subjects such as Christian doctrine, Latin, Greek, Old Irish, history (including medieval), geography, French literature, English, modern languages (French, German, Italian and Spanish), experimental science (chemistry and physics), mathematics (arithmetic, algebra, geometry and trigonometry), nature studies, physical science, book-keeping, gardening/elementary agriculture, Egyptology, archaeology, drawing, handwriting, manual instruction, philosophy, phonetics, elocution, hygiene and first aid, short-hand, typewriting, dancing, physical drill and music (vocal and instrumental). Half-holiday lectures, often illustrated by magic lantern, were delivered by eminent visiting speakers, including Douglas Hyde, Edward Martyn, Standish O'Grady, Mary Hayden, Pádraic Colum, Agnes O'Farrelly, Eoin MacNeill, Roger Casement, Alice Stopford Green and W.B. Yeats. These speakers lectured on a variety of subjects, such as literature, art, physics, philosophy, classics, science, phonetics, horticulture, and Irish and general history.

Patrick believed that the education or instruction of a child should not be limited to the classroom. In addition to lectures, the students visited art galleries, museums, the Zoo and the Botanic Gardens. The school was well equipped with facilities, including a small gymnasium where gymnastics and drill were taught. Gaelic football, hurling and handball were the main outdoor games played by the students, while chess was the most popular indoor game. Irish was the official language of the school and the preferred language of communication between teachers and students. This policy also applied to the preparatory school where Margaret and her assistant, Gertrude Bloomer, welcomed thirty boys and girls in its first year. Though only one of their students spoke Irish as their native language, the other children received instruction in Irish, albeit 'cautiously employed' in nature studies, arithmetic and drill, from their first day at school.[7]

In the school year 1909–10, the number of students enrolled at St Enda's rose to *c.*130; about thirty boarders, seventy day pupils and thirty in the preparatory school (which then only accepted boys). Patrick noted that, of the seventy boys enrolled for the 1909/10 school year, there was hardly any student who did 'not come from a home which has traditions of work and sacrifice for Ireland, traditions of literary, scholarly or political service'.[8] The children and relatives of prominent figures such as Eoin MacNeill, D.P. Moran, Agnes O'Farrelly, Pádraic Colum, Stephen Gwynn and Seán T. O'Kelly attended St Enda's. While the school was growing in success, Pearse and Sons was experiencing a dramatic fall in commissions as a result of the general decline in the building trade. In 1910, the family decided to close the business. At the time of its dissolution, Pearse and Sons was valued at £500; this amount was later used to fund the relocation of the school to The Hermitage in Rathfarnham in September 1910.

The Hermitage, an eighteenth-century house, set in fifty acres of woods, orchards, a river and lake, appealed to Patrick as an ideal space to accommodate the school's growing numbers. He believed it was a more suitable setting for the school than Cullenswood House, where they were 'too much in the Suburban Groove'.[9] Extensive modifications costing £2,666 were carried out on The Hermitage to adapt it for the purpose of a school and a lease of £300 per annum was agreed. The move to Rathfarnham, however, was not successful. The number of students at St Enda's reduced from 130 in 1909–10 to approximately 70 in 1910–11. Rathfarnham was too far from Dublin city for many families and, unlike Cullenswood House, not accessible by tram. Considering the wonderful academic and athletic achievements gained at Cullenswood House in the school year 1909–10, Patrick later opined that, if he had believed in luck, he would never have moved to Rathfarnham. Nevertheless, the students who enrolled at The Hermitage revelled in their new environment and the homely atmosphere cultivated in the school by the Pearse family.

Each member of the Pearse family, and some of their extended family, taught at or assisted in the running of the school. Mrs Pearse's warm and maternal character suited her role as housekeeper and matron. She was a welcoming figure for the children and acted as a surrogate mother for homesick boarders, assisted in her domestic duties by her cousin, Margaret Mary Brady. From 1910 onwards, Margaret was an assistant mistress but also assumed various other roles, including teaching junior French and corresponding with pupils during holidays. Ruth Dudley Edwards noted that Margaret was 'a worrier, but conscientious and hardworking'; her involvement in the school suited her busy nature.[10] Former student Kenneth Reddin credited the Pearse women with the creation of a homelike atmosphere in the school, noting that St Enda's

> was completely un-institutional … neither that of a prison, a reformatory, nor a hospital. In fact at night we often went down to Mrs Pearse for a biscuit or, if that failed, for a slice of bread and a glass of milk, or to Miss Pearse or Miss Brady. That was the secret of the homely and non-institutional atmosphere of St Enda's. Women had charge of the domestic arrangements. If one wanted an extra blanket, one didn't have to interview an impersonal Lay

Brother, one went to Mrs Pearse, or Miss Pearse, and got it
… just as you might go to your mother for it.[11]

Mary Brigid took over the role of harp teacher from Owen
Lloyd in 1910, providing piano and voice lessons as part of the
extracurricular activities offered at the school. She also played the
harp at school events and participated in various plays. One of her
former students recalled that she 'did not have Margaret's steadiness
and could not handle classes as her sister could; she was more
adept at individual music classes'.[12] Although Margaret, her
mother and members of their extended family resided at The
Hermitage, Mary Brigid did not live with her family.

Initially, Willie worked part-time at St Enda's because he was
also studying at the Metropolitan School of Art, where he was
awarded a studentship from 1910 to 1912.[13] Between 1906 and
1913, he exhibited works at the Royal Hibernian Academy and
An tOireachtas, but still found time to teach art, English, history,
and geography. He was popular with the students, playing sports
with them, and assisting in school plays and the design of
stage sets for theatrical performances. Willie's nephew, Alfred
McGloughlin, who lived with the Pearses at St Enda's, also assisted
in the production of school plays and was described by Patrick as
a valuable member of 'Staff without Portfolio'.[14]

Students at St Enda's enjoyed both a stimulating intellectual
and cultural education. Drama was an important part of school
life; pageants, and plays written by Patrick, teachers at St Enda's
and contemporary playwrights, were performed at the school
and external venues such as the Abbey Theatre in Dublin and
the Castlebellingham Feis in Co. Louth. The students' first
performance took place on 20 March 1908 at the school
gymnasium as part of the school's St Enda's Day celebrations.
They performed *An Naomh ar Iarraidh* by Douglas Hyde and *The
Coming of Fionn* by Standish O'Grady to an audience of over one
hundred people. Thomas MacDonnell composed original music
and made arrangements of old airs to enhance the performance,

Willie designed the costumes and was assisted in the production of the pageant by Alfred. Newspaper reviews complimented the young thespians on their excellent delivery and convincing performances.

On 17 February 1910, Mary Brigid and Willie acted in *The School for Scandal* by Richard Brinsley Sheridan, which was presented as part of a social evening at St Enda's. In *The Home-Life*, Mary Brigid recalled an amusing incident that happened while she and Willie were producing Morgan O'Friel's *The Skull* at the school. Mary Brigid was dressed as a poor countrywoman for the role, her face was heavily made up and she was unrecognisable. Just before the curtain rose, Patrick entered the study hall and, looking at Mary Brigid, exclaimed, 'Who is this woman, and what does she want here?'[15] Willie shouted, 'Why, it's Mary Brigid!'[16] Patrick was overcome with a laughing fit and had to compose himself in another room before re-emerging to introduce the performance.

When St Enda's transferred to The Hermitage in 1910, Cullenswood House became the home of St Ita's/Scoil Íde, a bilingual senior day and boarding school for Catholic girls, set up by Patrick after requests from the families of boys attending St Enda's to establish an equivalent school for girls. Although Patrick established St Ita's, he had little involvement in the school's administration or curriculum. St Ita's shared similar educational objectives to that of St Enda's, namely to 'ground its pupils in sound, moral and religious principles, to train them in practical Christianity, and to awaken in them a spirit of patriotism and a sense of duty and obligation to their county'.[17] The girls received an education in the homely surroundings of Cullenswood House which was Irish in tone and employed bilingual methods of teaching. Every aspect of the girl's education and development was catered for, with special emphasis on their health and well-being, physical and personal development, and religious education. A number of places were also set aside for girls attending the National University.

Patrick was director (stiúrthóir) of St Ita's, Gertrude Bloomer (a musician and graduate of Cambridge University) was house mistress, Mary Cotter was assistant mistress, and there were three music teachers teaching Irish harp, strings, piano and voice. Other notable teachers included Louise Gavan Duffy, educationalist, nationalist and Irish language enthusiast, Willie Pearse and Mary Colum (née Gunning Maguire). A wide variety of subjects featured on the school curriculum of this bilingual school, including classics, English, French, German and sciences. The staff and students of St Enda's and St Ita's enjoyed a close working relationship. Mary Colum later observed that when she started teaching at St Ita's, she was already acquainted with many of the teachers at both schools as they were members of various popular contemporary cultural movements. She commented that '[t]he staff of Pearse's two schools were knit into all the casuses … [a]s in almost every other enterprise in Dublin of the period, an atmosphere of literature and art pervaded everything; many of the pupils came from writing and academic families.'[18]

Many of the visiting lecturers to St Enda's also delivered similar papers at St Ita's. Mary Bulfin (a former pupil of St Ita's and sister of Éamonn Bulfin, one of the first students enrolled at St Enda's) remembered Patrick's weekly visits to the school each Wednesday when he would speak to the girls on a variety of subjects including nature studies, Irish folklore and personal development. On one occasion, he spoke to the girls about his own school days, his weakest subjects at school and the merits of various professions. He advised the girls to choose professions which would showcase their skills and capabilities and make them happy.[19] These addresses had a lasting effect on Mary and her classmates at St Ita's and she considered Patrick 'a very great and marvellous person' whom she was never afraid to approach in times of difficulty.[20]

One such difficulty occured at a school céilí (dance) before Halloween. Irish dances were only permitted at céilís but the girls were eager to dance a waltz. They pleaded with Patrick to allow them to dance a waltz and, as a compromise, agreed to call the dance a two-handed reel. To the great surprise of the teachers in attendance, Patrick agreed, but insisted that the girls simply call it a waltz. The staff at St Ita's were amused by Patrick's pragmatism and candour.

St Ita's and St Enda's regularly collaborated on the organisation of céilís and production of dramas. One of their most successful productions was Patrick's Irish language version of *The Passion Play*, which was staged at the Abbey Theatre on 7 and 8 April 1911. Sixty boys and some of the staff from St Enda's joined with twenty girls from St Ita's for the performances. Thomas MacDonnell played the role of Jesus and, as in previous plays, he composed various pieces of music to accompany the play, including a choral piece for the boys during the opening scene of the play in the Garden of Gethsemane and a lament for the women standing at the foot of the cross on Calvary's hill. Willie assumed the role of Pontius Pilate, Thomas MacDonagh and Patrick were cast as the two thieves and Micheál MacRuaidhraí was transformed into a terrifying Barrabas. Patrick directed the play and only scheduled a couple of rehearsals: 'he seemed to have a divine belief that everyone would rise to the occasion and perform their individual parts adequately at the actual performance, no matter how woodenly they behaved at the rehearsals'.[21]

Nevertheless, the play was a success with the *Freeman's Journal* describing the performance as 'unique in the modern history of Dublin, and its approach is a matter of profound interest to all concerned with education or with the arts'.[22] Unfortunately, collaborations between the two schools were short-lived as St Ita's closed in June 1912 due to a lack of funds. Louise Gavin Duffy, who taught at the school, offered to take over the lease on the building but her offer was not accepted and she established Scoil Bhríde, her own Irish language school for girls, in 1917, in St Stephen's Green, Dublin. The building which housed St Ita's became a university hostel for girls.

Many of the staff who participated in plays at St Enda's were also involved in amateur dramatic societies in Dublin. Mary Brigid and Willie pursued their common interest in theatre and drama by forming the Leinster Stage Society in 1910. They enjoyed a close relationship, albeit not as strong as the one she and Patrick shared. Mary Brigid and Willie's common interest in theatre and drama developed steadily from their early forays as children in the drawing room of their home at Great Brunswick Street and later in Sandymount. The Leinster Stage Society was an amateur theatrical company that included their nephew Alfred, Desmond Ryan (a student/friend of Patrick's), the poet James Crawford Neil, sisters Máire Nic Shiúbhlaigh (Mary Walker) and Betty King, Mary Fitzgerald, Eileen O'Donahoe, Fred A. MacDonald, Florence Lehane, Samuel Lyons, Éamonn Bulfin, Sorley MacGarvey, Fred Holden, Tadhg Carleton, Morgan O'Friel, Miss M. Grant Cleary, Edwin P. Lewis, Lottie Welsh, Eva Jubb, Breffni O'Rorke, Julie Hayden, Maureen Nugent and Ella Delaney. They were all involved in various cultural movements of the period.

The Society's repertoire included many plays that were also performed at St Enda's: Standish O'Grady's *The Transformation of Fionn*, Daniel Corkery's *The Hermit and the King*, *Deirdre* by Æ, *The Skull* by Morgan O'Friel, *The Racing Lug* by J.H. Cousins and *For a Lady's Sake* and *The Rehearsal* by Sheamus O'Heran. The Leinster Stage Society was an important forum for Mary Brigid to showcase her writing skills. At least five original plays written by her formed part of the Society's repertoire. These included *The Message*, *Over the Stile* (see Appendix 3), *The Good People*, *The King's Ransome* and *Geese*. *The Message*, a play in one act with an epilogue, focuses on a young girl's imminent adoption by ladies from a local 'Big House'. Dónal, the local schoolmaster, strongly objects and appeals to the ladies not to take her. He cautions that, unlike the swallows who return every year, the little girl would not adapt socially to her salubrious new surroundings. In the end, the child is left with her own kin.

Over the Stile, a comedy in two scenes set around the central character, Pat Casey, incorporated a piece of music of her own composition called 'Peggy's Song'. *The Good People (A Plea for an*

Ancient Race), a comedy about the interaction of fairies with the Irish peasantry, was set in a fishing village near Dublin. A performance of this play in December 1911 was complimented for the 'charming and home-like fashion in which the plot [was] elucidated'.[23] The central character, Larry the fisherman, was played by Willie, and his 'considerable ability'[24] was commended in the newspapers. Mary Brigid also adapted several novellas/novels by Charles Dickens for performance, including *The Chimes* (novella), *The Cricket on the Hearth* (novella), *Barnaby Rudge* (historical novel) and 'The Baron of Grogzwig' (part of *Nicholas Nickleby*, a ghost story).

The first performance of the Leinster Stage Society was on 27 May 1910 in the Abbey Theatre, with another performance on 28 May. Alfred McGloughlin's comic farce, *The Countess of Strasbourg* received its premiere. The play, which was set in an inn on the outskirts of Ulm, Southern Germany, on the evening of 5 October 1805, centres on a battle between Austrian and French forces to capture the town of Ulm – the French army eventually prevails. Willie played the lead role of Napoleon, with Éamonn Bulfin from St Enda's as Marshal Ney and Sorley MacGarvey as the Austrian General Klenau. The Society also performed Mary Brigid's *Over the Stile* and *The Message* and premièred O'Grady's *The Transformation of Fionn* with Willie in the title role and Éamonn Bulfin as a warrior. In February 1911, the Society presented plays by Æ, James H. Cousins, Alfred, and Mary Brigid at the Abbey Theatre. Mary Brigid and Alfred acted along with Alfred's future wife, Marcella Dowling, whose brothers attended St Enda's. The performances were well attended and 'there was not only enthusiastic applause from a considerable audience, but sundry calls'.[25] The theatre critic Jack Point wrote that '[t]he Leinster Stage Society is a theatrical combination with which the Dublin play-going public is unfamiliar. After last night's performance it is safe to say more will be heard of it in future.'[26]

Encouraged by these positive reviews, the Society booked the Abbey for further performances towards the end of 1911. On 26

December 1911 the Society introduced two new plays to their repertoire at the Abbey, namely Mary Brigid's comedy *The Good People* and O'Heran's *For a Lady's Sake*. The Society also performed on 31 December and included Corkery's one act play, *The Hermit and the King*. The cast for both shows included Crawford Neil, Fred A. McDonald, Frank Walker and Mary Fitzgerald. On 1 January 1912, the members of the Society again graced the stage of the Abbey Theatre with performances of *The Hermit and the King*, *The Good People*, *The Skull*, and *For a Lady's Sake*.

The following month, on 5 February 1912, the Society celebrated the centenary of Charles Dickens's birth with the performance of a special adaptation of 'Baron of Grogzwig' from *Nicholas Nickleby*. Despite drawing attention to the Society's incorrect date of Dickens's birth (the correct date is 7 February), the reviewer from the *Irish Times* commented on the 'entertaining passages of dialogue', the strong performances throughout and the considerable talent of the lead actor, Fred Loco, in Mary Brigid's adaptations.[27] Willie was cast as the lead in the second play, *The Cricket on the Hearth*. It featured 'delightful touches of pathos and pleasant – if sometimes rather boisterous – passages of humour … the acting was of a high standard, and showed the work of the Society in a very favourable light'.[28] Music for the production was provided by members of the Pioneer Orchestra and mandolinist Harry D'Arcy.

Following their acclaimed performances at the Abbey Theatre from 1911–12, the Society's committee decided to book the Opera House in Cork for one week in May 1912 to perform a variety of plays from their repertoire, including Mary Brigid's adaptations of works by Dickens and plays by McGloughlin, O'Friel and Corkery. Willie hoped that all profits from the run would be contributed to St Enda's. The run, however, was an artistic and financial disaster for the Society. Mary Brigid, Willie and their mother, Máire Nic Shiúlbhlaigh and her sister Patricia Walker, Desmond Ryan, Máire Hughes and James Crawford Neil travelled to Cork to perform. Despite the attendance and support of prominent local cultural nationalists, such as Terence MacSwiney, Con O'Leary and Daniel Corkery, performances by the Society were poorly received. Desmond Ryan reported that the performances were savaged by local critics with one reviewer even commenting that the voice of the prompter was louder than those of the actors.

Ryan wrote the following about the horrendous experience:

> every day the Opera House door-keeper cheered the company for the small audiences thus: 'It's all over the town that your show is a rotten show. The whole town know it's a rotten show, man. You have to be careful of what you bring down here from Dublin or anywhere else. Why, we criticise the very choruses of operas, man.'[29]

Several years later, Máire Nic Shiúbhlaigh recalled in her memoirs that even a young boy selling the *Echo* newspaper in Cork refused a free ticket to a performance.[30] The Society was forced to seek financial assistance from Patrick to settle debts at the theatre, and further plans to tour and raise funds for St Enda's were cancelled. The Society ceased all performances thereafter and the Leinster Stage Society was officially wound up in late 1912.

The Cork fiasco was indicative of how reliant the Pearse siblings were on Patrick, both financially and for moral support. Over the next few years, however, as Patrick became increasingly focused on political matters, he had fewer opportunities to engage with his family's interests. Although his friendship with Willie would strengthen in the years before the Rising, his relationships with Mary Brigid and Margaret often suffered as he single-mindedly pursued his dream of achieving an autonomous Irish-speaking nation.

CHAPTER 4

Surviving the Rising

All the light and joy of life seemed to have gone from us in those few minutes.[1]

Margaret Pearse

Although the family were committed to running St Enda's during term time, they enjoyed their time away from school life on holidays in Connemara, Co. Galway, and Killarney, Co. Kerry. Patrick loved the scenery and ambience of the West of Ireland. He purchased land in Rosmuc in 1905 and a cottage was built there in 1909 to accommodate family holidays. Mary Brigid did not share her brother's love of the West which was too wild and desolate for her. Killarney was her preferred holiday destination, being unsurpassed, she believed, for sheer beauty. She often argued this point with Patrick: 'I maintain – as I *still* maintain – that Killarney is unsurpassed for sheer beauty; he would have it that "The Twelve Pins" in his beloved Connemara district beat the Long Range, Killarney – ay, and even the Gap of Dunloe – hollow! I was not convinced.'[2]

To settle their dispute, they decided to travel down to his thatched cottage in Rosmuc. This short holiday turned out to be a horrific experience for Mary Brigid and the entire Pearse family. The journey began with an arduous train ride from Dublin during which a group of 'wholsome [sic], buxum, but loquacious

Galway Fisherwomen' boarded the train with baskets of fish.[3] Their constant chatter irritated Mary Brigid, who was suffering from anxiety, or, as she described it, 'bordering on a complete nervous breakdown'.[4] From the moment she arrived in Rosmuc, everything about the environment was challenging for her, even the overpowering smell of turf. She later explained, 'nerves are tricky things, and very often the sights and scents we really like effect our nerves adversely'.[5]

During the holiday, Patrick made every effort to alleviate his sister's distress. He sent regular telegrams to her doctor in Dublin, keeping him abreast of her condition and requesting medication to be sent via the post offices at Maam Cross and Rosmuc. Mary Brigid was particular about the type of food she ate, and Patrick often cycled for miles to source 'bakers' bread' or fresh fruit. She appreciated his efforts and later noted that '[l]ooking back on this time I can still marvel at the eveness of temper and unruffled good humour which my brother displayed in such trying circumstances'.[6]

Patrick sold his cottage to Margaret for £10 in 1912 to relieve his debts at St Enda's, but the family continued to holiday there, often with relations, friends and students of St Enda's. In July 1915, the entire Pearse family, their cousin, Margaret Brady and Desmond Ryan enjoyed an extended holiday at the cottage. It was during this trip that Patrick wrote and rehearsed the oration that he delivered at Jeremiah O'Donovan Rossa's graveside at Glasnevin Cemetery on 1 August 1915. O'Donovan Rossa spent many years in prison in England following a conviction for his part in the failed Fenian Rising of 1865. Margaret, Patrick, Willie and Mary Brigid fondly remembered their mother and Auntie Margaret singing ballads to them in their childhood about the exploits of O'Donovan Rossa. Almost three decades later, their mother proudly accompanied her two sons back to Dublin from Rosmuc in advance of what would become one of the most significant events in Patrick's life.

Patrick's writings and speeches from the early 1910s onwards reveal an evolution in his political thinking, from constitutional to militant nationalism. His O'Donovan Rossa oration was the culmination of years of political speechmaking that began with the Robert Emmet Commemoration on 6 March 1911, in which he impressed veteran Fenian Tom Clarke, who had hitherto questioned Patrick's brand of nationalism. The following year, on 31 March, Patrick appeared on a platform at a Home Rule rally alongside John Redmond, Eoin MacNeill and Joseph Devlin. In his speech, Patrick defended the Third Home Rule Bill (introduced on 11 April 1912, though suspended) but threatened that, if the Bill was not passed, Britain would be met 'with violence and the edge of the sword'.[7] Patrick's increasing prominence at high-profile political gatherings resulted in an invitation to deliver an address at Wolfe Tone's grave in Bodenstown Cemetery on 22 June 1913. This address helped to endear him to members of the Irish Republican Brotherhood (IRB), who had previously been divided on his potential recruitment.

Patrick joined the Irish Volunteer Force in 1913 and was sworn into the IRB by Bulmer Hobson in December. In February 1914, he embarked on a lecture tour of America to fundraise for St Enda's where he raised over $3,000. When he returned to Ireland in May, he was wholly committed to militant nationalism. He was greatly impressed by John Devoy and other members of Clan na Gael during his US visit and he declared that, irrespective of whether Home Rule was passed or not, nationhood could only be achieved through armed resistance.

Patrick's increasing involvement in political activism affected his commitment to St Enda's. The number of students dropped considerably from seventy in 1914–15 to approximately thirty in 1915–16. Vacant dormitories were occupied by past pupils who lived there while attending courses at university. In the school year 1915–16, there were five full-time teachers at the school; Frank Burke, Pádraic Óg Ó Conaire, Peter Slattery, Patrick and Willie. Margaret taught classes in Christian doctrine and Mary Brigid taught music. From early 1915 onwards, St Enda's was increasingly used as a centre for planning and preparation of a revolution. A small shooting range was erected at the back of the school in early 1915 and members of the 'E' Company, 4th Battalion Dublin Brigade (known as 'Pearse's Own') practiced there. Members of the 3rd Battalion of this company also practiced each Sunday in Cullenswood House under the direction of Paddy Doyle. The 4th Battalion took part in regular field exercises, route marches, parades and target practice in wooded areas on the grounds of St Enda's. A military drill organised by the Irish Volunteers took place in September 1915 at St Enda's alongside shooting competitions and field manoeuvres exhibited by Cumann na mBan.[8] As well as intensive training, a substantial amount of ammunition, including bullets and hand grenades, was produced by teachers and former students living at the school under the direction of chemistry teacher, Peter Slattery.[9]

This increased military activity did not go unnoticed by several parents, some of whom removed their children from the school. Although Margaret and her mother were not directly involved in preparations for the revolution, they knew that ammunition and weaponry were being stored at St Enda's. Margaret later recalled her relief when, on St Patrick's Day 1916, several Volunteers stayed at St Enda's to guard the ammunition while she and a number of students attended a special mass for the Volunteers at SS Michael and John's Church, Essex Quay.[10] She was also concerned for Patrick's safety at this time. In early April 1916, Patrick confided in her that he feared he was being watched by Sergeant Harris of the Royal Irish Constabulary (RIC) at Rathfarnham Station.[11] As a consequence, he did not act as sponsor for the boys who received Confirmation that year and asked Willie to act as sponsor instead.[12]

The school closed early for Easter holidays and, by Palm Sunday, as Margaret noted, 'those preparing for battle were free of school duties and responsibilities.'[13] Margaret and her mother were aware of the plans for insurrection; the extent of this knowledge is not known, but they knew Patrick and Willie were prepared to die for their political beliefs. There is no evidence to indicate whether Mary Brigid knew any details of her brothers' intentions; given her delicate nature and the fact that she did not live at St Enda's, it is unlikely the family shared any information with her.

St Enda's was a hive of activity the week before the Rising. There were many visitors to the school and Liam Mellows, who had escaped from Reading Gaol, was hiding out there, disguised as a priest. Frank Burke, a former student and later principal of the school, 'watched vans and cars arrive every day for a week collecting boxes of grenades, rifles and bullets and ferrying them to different destinations'.[14] Military preparations, however, did not entirely dominate life at St Enda's that week. On Monday, 17 April 1916, Margaret, Mrs Pearse, Patrick, Willie, Liam Mellows, Éamonn and Áine Ceannt and their son Rónán (a student at St Enda's) enjoyed lunch together. Áine Ceannt later remembered that there was no discussion of a planned revolution on that occasion.[15]

The events of the days leading up to the Rising were described in detail in several accounts by Margaret.[16] She recalled when Patrick told her about the devastating news of the failed landing of the *Aud* at Fenit, Co. Kerry, on Good Friday (21 April 1916):

> I can remember well when the terrible tragic news came from Kerry. In the room where I am now writing, my brother Pat was sitting, silent, stricken as it were with the import of the message just received. I asked him if the tragic occurrence would make any serious difference in his plans. He replied: 'Yes, a terrible difference.'[17]

The *Libau* ('Aud'), a German cargo vessel under the command of Captain Karl Spindler, was carrying 20,000 rifles, 10 machine guns, and explosives destined for the Irish Volunteers; it was disguised as a Norwegian freighter carrying a cargo of wood. The vessel arrived earlier than planned and was intercepted by HMS *Bluebell* of the Royal Navy. Roger Casement, Robert Monteith and Sergeant Daniel Bailey (alias Beverley) who were awaiting the arrival of the arms vessel on their submarine U19, came ashore on a dinghy at Banna Strand. Casement was arrested at McKenna's Fort, near Banna Strand, and Monteith and Bailey went on the run. Bailey was later arrested in Tralee, while Monteith escaped to Cork.

Late on the night of Good Friday, the Pearse family had retired to bed when Eoin MacNeill called to St Enda's; Patrick and Willie were due to accompany their mother to the Holy Saturday ceremony but these plans had to be cancelled. Before Patrick left with MacNeill, he asked Margaret about the times of alternative church ceremonies in the city centre. When Patrick returned the next day (Easter Saturday), Margaret noted his exhaustion and anxiety:

> … towards one or two o'clock he returned, looking weary and worn out. He spoke to our cousin saying: 'I'm nearly dead. Get me a cup of tea. I've had nothing since supper last night.' Whilst a hastily prepared breakfast was placed before him, he and I chatted, my first question being as to where he had received Holy Communion. He replied: 'In Dominick St. The ceremonies and Mass were over, but I asked the priest; at first he hesitated, but then seemed to change his mind and [said] it was all right.'[18]

Margaret observed that her brothers were reluctant to leave St Enda's on Easter Saturday night. One load of ammunition had not been collected and it was decided that Willie should remain with it. Dr Kathleen Lynn soon arrived in her car to collect the ammunition and transport it to Liberty Hall. Éamonn Bulfin followed behind her on his bicycle, having disguised the number plate of her car with mud. As the moment arrived for Patrick and Willie's departure, their mother and Margaret accompanied them to the gates of St Enda's where they said their goodbyes sadly and quickly so as not to attract attention. Mrs Pearse's parting words to her sons confirmed her support for their ideals: 'God be with you both. If we never meet here again, we'll meet in Heaven.'[19]

The following morning, Easter Sunday, Margaret, her mother and some of the boys from St Enda's attended morning mass in the Church of the Annunciation, Rathfarnham. It had been arranged that the Volunteers would meet outside the church after mass to attend military manoeuvres. Many had read Eoin MacNeill's countermanding order in the *Sunday Independent* and were confused. Margaret and her mother waited at the church for Éamonn Bulfin to accompany them back to St Enda's in their pony and trap. Bulfin eventually arrived back having refused a request by MacNeill and Seán Fitzgibbon to deliver dispatches about the cancellation of the Rising; Frank Connolly, another of the St Enda's university boys, was eventually tasked with carrying the dispatches.[20] When they arrived back at St Enda's, breakfast was delayed until the return of Joe Sweeney, who had left early that morning to receive Confession. When Sweeney arrived, Margaret recalled his fury at the poster cancelling the planned manoeuvres for that day. Sweeney was particularly angered by MacNeill declaring himself Chief of Staff of the Irish Volunteers. He believed that Patrick, or Pete as they affectionately referred to him, was 'the Chief'.[21]

Having received no further orders, Bulfin decided to travel to Liberty Hall to meet Patrick and obtain instructions for everyone anxiously waiting at St Enda's. Patrick ordered the boys to stand to arms and await his and Willie's return. Pat and Willie returned at about 6.00pm. The family dined together and, as dusk approached, the brothers left St Enda's for the last time; this time, they said their good-byes at the hall door. Margaret remembered that Patrick hesitated as they came to the hall and went back to retrieve something he had forgotten: 'Mother asked him: "Did you find it?" One word only did he reply: "Yes." It was the last word I remember to have heard him speak. I noticed he said it slowly and rather wearily. No doubt there were a few parting words, but all I recollect is that one word: "Yes."'[22]

On the morning of Easter Monday, the Volunteers at St Enda's received their much-awaited orders. They bade farewell to Margaret and Mrs Pearse and proceeded to the GPO in Dublin city centre. At some stage during that morning, Mary Brigid, hitherto unaware of plans for an insurrection, discovered the true extent of her brothers' involvement. She is reputed to have made her way to the city centre, met her brother, and pleaded with him, 'come home, Pat, and leave all this foolishness!'[23] From St Enda's, Margaret and her mother witnessed the fires engulfing Dublin during Easter week. Patrick and Willie sent Margaret and their mother a dispatch from the GPO informing them that the former students from St Enda's had acquitted themselves admirably and not to be concerned about their welfare.

On Sunday, 30 April, Margaret and her mother heard of the order to surrender. For a few days they received no information about the whereabouts of Patrick and Willie. At 10.00am on 3 May, a Capuchin priest, Fr Aloysius Travers, informed them that Patrick had been executed along with Thomas MacDonagh and Tom Clarke at 3.45 that morning. Margaret described hearing the devastating news as if 'all the light and joy of life seemed to have gone from us in those few minutes'.[24] She wrote:

> The day passed somehow and towards midnight we were aroused from an attempt to get a few hour's rest by the arrival of a military lorry. I went to the hall-door and was given a note saying that the prisoner, William Pearse, desired to see us. At once I realised we were to lose Willie. I returned to the bedroom, and said to mother: "More bad news. Willie wants to see us, so he is going too."[25]

At midnight, a military lorry arrived at St Enda's to bring Margaret and her mother to Kilmainham Gaol to bid farewell to Willie. Unfortunately, the lorry broke down *en route* and there was a further delay escorting them to Willie's cell. When Margaret later recounted the events of that day, she made no mention of

Mary Brigid joining her and her mother. She recalled that she and her mother were not afforded any privacy in Willie's cell as three military officers remained throughout their visit.[26] Willie told his mother and sister that while he was being transferred from Richmond Barracks to Kilmainham Gaol to meet Patrick before his execution, he believed he heard the fatal shots that ended his brother's life. Margaret and her mother assured Willie that they were proud of his actions and they believed the Rising was justified. The interview finished and they 'bade Willie a last good-bye, and left him gazing after us, one longing, sad look, till the cell door closed'.[27] They were anxious that Willie would receive a priest before his execution and pleaded with the guard to send one. Although Margaret doubted this would happen, Fr Augustine Hayden from the Capuchin Friary was permitted to pray with Willie before he was brought for execution. As the two women left the prison, they were handed some of Patrick's effects, but several documents written by him were withheld.

After the Rising, 3,509 people were arrested countrywide (with 1,486 released after questioning), 1,863 were deported and interned without trial in England (under the Defence of the Realm Act), and 171 were court-martialled, 90 of whom were sentenced to death. In all, 485 people lost their lives, over half of whom were civilians; c.2,614 people were injured and an estimated £2 million of property damaged. General Maxwell, who had taken command on Thursday, 28 April, ordered that a mass grave large enough to fit one hundred bodies be dug at Arbour Hill Prison, Dublin. The general feeling in Britain was that a revolution during a low point in the First World War was the ultimate treason; Maxwell was adamant that the perpetrators should be dealt stern justice. The military executions of the fourteen leaders of the Rising took place in Kilmainham Gaol, Dublin between 3 and 12 May 1916; they included five former teachers at St Enda's, namely Patrick, Willie, Thomas MacDonagh, Joseph Plunkett and Con Colbert.[28] The men were shot in the Stonebreakers' Yard and their bodies brought to Arbour Hill Prison, where they were interred without funeral rites or coffins and covered in quicklime. Public opinion, initially horrified by the destruction of Dublin city centre, turned in favour of the men.

Margaret and her mother petitioned for the bodies of Patrick and Willie to be returned to the family so that they could be buried in consecrated ground. The families of each man executed made similar requests. It seems, however, that Maxwell had decided the manner of their burial prior to the executions and sent a telegram to the United Kingdom's Liberal prime minister, Herbert Asquith, urging him not to return the bodies to their families. Maxwell insisted that the graves would be turned into shrines and would only attract further nationalist sympathy. Kathleen Clarke, Tom Clarke's wife, suspected that the bodies would never be returned. On the eve of her husband's execution, she asked to be notified after his death so she could claim his body and send it for burial: 'when you have wreaked your vengeance on him and taken his life, the body becomes mine'.[29] The officer on duty claimed he was unsure if the bodies of the executed men would be released. Bishop Edward O'Dwyer of Limerick, who had hitherto been unsympathetic to the nationalist cause, wrote a personal letter to Maxwell harshly criticising him for ignoring pleas for mercy and declaring that his regime was 'one of the worst and blackest chapters in the history of the misgovernment of the country'.[30]

After Easter 1916, Mrs Pearse and her daughter found themselves catapulted into the public and political domain, a heretofore unfamiliar space. There was no opportunity to grieve properly for Patrick and Willie or to come to terms with the bruality of their deaths. For the remainder of their lives, Margaret and her mother lived in the public gaze. In public, both women repeatedly iterated their belief that the Rising was justfied and that from the sacrifice of Patrick, Willie and their compatriots, a new nation would be born. It was not until the 1940s that Margaret wrote in some detail about her views on the Rising and on her brothers' actions. It was, quite simply, 'tragic but glorious'[31]

and from 1916 until her death in 1968, she adhered vehemently
to this belief. Margaret insisted that, despite the great loss
experienced by her and her family, they took comfort in the fact
that Patrick and Willie would spend eternity together. This
language of sacrifice and selflessness pervades all of her writings
on her family and the events of Easter 1916. For example, in the
Capuchin Annual of 1942, she wrote:

> Though our sorrow and our loss were very great indeed
> we were resigned Pat and Willie, so wonderfully united in
> life, were also united in death. We knew that God in His
> loving mercy had re-united them in an eternity of
> happiness, and that He in His own good time would grant
> from the sacrifice of 1916 a glorious fruition.[32]

Each execution irrevocably changed the home lives of the
families involved. Many of their homes and businesses were raided
repeatedly after the Rising, resulting in the traumatisation of
women and children. Unlike some of the wives and female
relatives of the executed leaders who had partipicated in the
Rising, Margaret and her mother took no part and were not
members of Cumann na mBan. In the immediate aftermath of
the Rising, Kathleen Clarke, with the assistance of members of
Cumann na mBan, established the Irish Republican Prisoners'
Dependants' Fund to support the families of those killed or
imprisoned. She had been entrusted by the IRB with the sum of
£3,000 for this purpose. It soon became apparent, however, that
this was an inadequate amount of money for the relief of the
families of the thousands of men arrested and interned.
Consequently, the Fund attempted to mount an appeal in various
newspapers but these were refused by the Censor on the grounds
that the title of the organisation included the word 'republican',
which was deemed offensive because it was regarded as anti-
monarchist. After eleven days, the name of the organisation was
changed to the Irish Volunteer Dependants' Fund.

Meanwhile, the Irish Parliamentary Party set up their own fund, the Irish National Aid Fund, which had similar objectives. These two organisations later merged to form the Irish National Aid and Volunteers' Dependants' Fund (INAVDF).[33] Kathleen Clarke was reluctant about the merger and questioned the motives of Redmond and his colleagues. She was eventually convinced to comply following visits from Mrs Pearse, Eamonn Ceannt's widow, Áine, and Archdeacon Murphy, a representative of Clan na Gael. Clarke was then tasked with selecting a committee and she deliberately chose female relatives of the executed men, many of whom were members of Cumann na mBan. The only exception was Mrs Pearse, whom Clarke believed 'had never been in anything outside her home before, and at times ... was bewildered'.[34] By August 1916, the committee of the INAVDF had collected approximately £27,000 through various fundraising initiatives.

Mrs Pearse became an important national figurehead after the execution of her sons. She and Margaret visited Irish prisoners of war at various English jails in June 1916. Mrs Pearse saw it as her duty to visit the prisoners, commenting that 'I must do my bit'.[35] At least sixteen past pupils of St Enda's took part in the Rising, eight of whom were interned at Frongoch Internment Camp in Wales: Desmond Ryan, Joseph Sweeney, Joseph O'Connor, John Kilgallon, Frank Burke, Éamonn Bulfin, Brian Joyce and Fintan Murphy. Two employees at St Enda's, Patrick Donnelly and Micheál Mac Ruaidhrí (the gardener), were also sent to Frongoch. In a letter to Eugene Cronin, a former student at St Enda's, Margaret wrote that the prisoners were generally treated well, except in Dartmoor Prison where Peter Slattery and former student Conor McGinley were imprisoned.[36]

Before Mrs Pearse departed for England, she met with Laurence Nugent and his wife, Dr O'Kelly and Fintan Murphy Snr on 7 May to discuss the possibility of reopening the school. She was persuaded that reopening the school would be the most fitting tribute to her sons. Margaret initially opposed the proposal stating candidly, '[p]ersonally I don't want it, but the Irish in America and England wish it so we do not like to hinder the good work'.[37] Offers of financial assistance were immediately forthcoming, particularly from private individuals and associations in Britain and North America who were sympathetic to the political ideologies of Patrick Pearse and were eager to show their solidarity with the Pearse family. In mid–May, Passionist priest and family friend Fr Eugene Nevin wrote to Mrs Pearse suggesting she accept an offer of financial help from a syndicate in London to support 'the national sanctuary consecrated by the glorious work' initiated by Patrick.[38]

In the autumn of 1916, St Enda's was reopened at Cullenswood House (the original location of the school) because The Hermitage was occupied by British soldiers. A small committee was established to manage the financial affairs of the school and it opened with fifteen boarders and a small number of day pupils, including a number of students who were enrolled before the Rising. Sons of executed leaders, Michael Mallin, Éamonn Ceannt and Tom Clarke were also enrolled and their fees were paid by the INAVDF. The Pearse family received £1,750 from the INAVDF between October 1917 and March 1918, some of which was used to fund grants or scholarships for students. Joseph MacDonagh (brother of Thomas) was appointed headmaster, but after his rearrest in late 1917, he was replaced by Peter Slattery and later by Frank Burke, who remained as headmaster until 1935. Many of those who assumed teaching roles at St Enda's after the Rising were past pupils of the school or had taken part in the Rising. Mary Bulfin, Seán Beaumont and Frank Connolly also taught intermittently at the school.

Cullenswood House, however, was not solely a centre for the education of St Enda's students. Michael Collins had an office there and Desmond Ryan, Éamonn Bulfin, Fintan Murphy and others, who reorganised the Rathfarnham Company of the Irish Volunteers in early 1917, concealed ammunition in the walls of the house. Margaret and her mother were not entirely aware of the extent of the caché stored there, so when Margaret decided to fly a tricolour over Cullenswood in an act of defiance against British troops stationed at The Hermitage, Collins promptly removed the flag so as to avoid attracting the attention of the police.[39]

From the moment St Enda's reopened in 1916 until its doors closed in 1935, Margaret and her mother struggled to run the school. Before the Rising, Patrick was an integral part of the day-to-day running of St Enda's, his mother had worked as the school's housekeeper and Margaret taught religious education and French. Now they had to accept additional financial and administrative roles and were often out of their depth. The family, together with past pupils, supporters and the INAVDF, purchased Cullenswood House after its lease expired. Three trustees were put in place to oversee the management of the school, namely Louise Gavan Duffy and Alfred McLoughlin, on behalf of the INAVDF, and Laurence Nugent, representing Mrs Pearse. St Enda's returned to The Hermitage after Easter holidays in 1919. When Patrick signed the lease on The Hermitage on 15 July 1910, there was an option to purchase the property by 1 July 1920. As that date was fast approaching, a fundraising campaign was organised in the USA to purchase the property on Mrs Pearse's behalf. The money was raised by the American Save St Enda's Fund and The Hermitage became the property of Mrs Pearse in December 1920.

Following the purchase, various committees were put in place to deal with financial and educational matters at the school. Mrs Pearse and her daughter resented their control. Mrs Pearse believed that her role was being undermined and, in a letter to a friend, wrote that she had given 'all she possessed to save *it* [St Enda's] for the Irish Nation ... But if this sacrifice of mine made in good faith ... cannot be carried out on my sincere ideas better not be carried out at all.'[40] It should be noted that, although members of the Pearse family drew only a fraction of the money owed to them for their work at the school, they struggled to keep the school going financially.

During the turbulent period 1919–21, Pearse properties were targeted by various groups hoping to find weaponry and ammunition concealed therein. Cullenswood House was routinely raided by British military forces, but, according to one eye witness account, a raid in the early hours of the morning on 30 January 1921 left the house in 'a regular ruin'.[41] Officers arrived in uniform in armoured cars and lorries. They broke every window with pickaxes, pulled up hundreds of feet of flooring, smashed the greenhouses, chimney pots, roof slates, furniture, fireplaces and started a fire. Mrs Pearse sued for damages of £3,600 through her solicitors Messrs Reddin and Reddin in March 1921, but the Recorder's Court decided the act was not malicious and her case was subsequently dismissed. Patrick's cottage in Rosmuc was also targeted by the Black and Tans in 1921. Margaret successfully sued the British authorities for damage to this property and received £200 in compensation in 1925.

Even in the early years of the Irish Free State, Margaret and her mother were subjected to frequent searches of St Enda's by Free State soldiers.[42] At 10.30pm on 12 July 1922, Margaret accompanied the soldiers during their search of the house insisting they 'Come on, search away. We are used to the British, but this is our first time to be searched by Irish traitors.'[43] Mrs Pearse reminded the soldiers that they were wearing similar uniforms to those worn by her sons when they fought for an independent Ireland, not a Free State. She accused them of behaving like Black and Tans and was disgusted that men such as Michael Collins and Richard Mulcahy, whom she had protected and supported in Cullenswood House for many years, had betrayed her so callously and completely.

From June to September 1924, Mrs Pearse toured the USA to raise funds for St Enda's and Sinn Féin. This tour of cities such as Boston, New York, Concorde, Lexington and Detroit was arduous for a 67-year-old woman, but was a testament to her desperation to keep the doors of St Enda's open. The trip raised $10,000, a substantial amount. Throughout the 1920s, donations were sent to the Pearses from all parts of the world; for example $100 from the Pittsburgh Irish Independence Club; £100 from Éamonn Bulfin's school in Lima, Peru and $1,500 from a group of Irish Americans represented by Eugene Kinkaid. Some Gaelic Athletic Association (GAA) clubs in Mitchelstown, Co. Cork and Limerick organised fundraising matches and an annual céilí was held in New York City to raise funds. The main source of funds was from the USA and Canada, so in 1926, Margaret embarked on a fundraising tour to the USA.

In the absence of proper records, it is impossible to say how much money was donated to Mrs Pearse and Margaret from 1916 onwards and also how this income was spent. The donations were sporadic, however, and the financial situation at St Enda's was precarious throughout the 1920s and 30s. In a letter to the McGraths from Long Island, New York, in 1927, Margaret expressed her concerns about her mother's health and the endless work and financial strain they were both under. She told them, 'I never get one free hour, the work and worry are greater than ever ... [w]ork is going well here and I have many plans for the welfare of the school, but the financial strain is terrible and entirely too much for mother. She is not at all well and seems quite unfit for the struggle to keep things going.'[44]

Notwithstanding this, Mrs Pearse perservered with her efforts to keep St Enda's open. In 1928, she received a letter from the Department of Defence regarding the Army Pensions Board's awarding of a weekly pension of £2 in respect of the death of Patrick together with a weekly sum of £1 backdated to 1922. In her response, she reminded them that her claim was for two executed sons and that her situation was unlike that of other families of executed leaders. She had no sons to provide for her in old age and her problems were compounded by the fact that she had an invalided daughter. She wrote, '[m]y delicate daughter, Mary Brigid, is a complete invalid, now dependent entirely on me, after twelve years hard struggle in writing stories and teaching music. I would willingly give you a full account of my financial difficulties, if this is necessary to support my claim, but I cannot believe that the Ministry of Finance has sanctioned such a paltry offer to me.'[45]

Despite Mrs Pearse's dogged determination to keep St Enda's open as a living memorial to her two sons, the general consensus amongst friends and colleagues was that they should close the school. In 1928, Fr Denis Fahey, a Spiritan priest from Rockwell College, Co. Tipperary (and friend of Éamon de Valera), wrote to Margaret advising her to close the school. He believed that the stress of running St Enda's was having a negative affect on Mrs Pearse's health and that she deserved 'to have a chance of passing the remaining years of her life in peace'.[46] He suggested that Margaret, although nobly committed to her brother's educational project, was blinded by a sense of duty and loyalty, and the closure of the school was the only option.

These sentiments were echoed in government circles. A bilingual school, espousing a Gaelic ethos, should have appealed to successive governments endeavouring to promote Irish language and culture in education, but consistent pleas for adequate and regular financial support for St Enda's were ignored. Finance Minister Ernest Blythe reiterated the government's trenchant stance that no special case could or would be made for St Enda's. In August 1931, Blythe wrote:

> While we all agree that Sgoil [sic] Éanna has special claims, there is serious objection to helping it by means of special Government grants. As you are doubtless aware there are at the moment in the neighbourhood of 90 schools in Class A, B1 and B2 of the Secondary programme and of this number about 48 are in the first two classes and are doing particularly good work in Irish. If a special grant were given to Sgoil Éanna it is felt that all, or at least the great majority of these institutions, would press for similar treatment which could hardly be witheld. The 24 A Schools, in which Irish is the ordinary medium of

instruction in all subjects excepting modern languages, would feel themselves particularly aggrieved if one B2 school, no matter what its history, were given larger grants. In the circumstances I regret that it is not possible to make provision in the manner suggested.[47]

Despite the close connection between Éamon de Valera, leader of Fianna Fáil, and the Pearse family, Mrs Pearse's personal appeals to him to use his influence to get funding for the school were fruitless. In a letter from de Valera's private secretary, Maurice Moynihan, to Mrs Pearse in July 1932, he informed her of de Valera's view that the school could not continue to operate at a loss and that it should be closed and converted into a preparatory college or university hostel.[48] Perhaps, as Brendan Walsh has suggested, '[h]ad Pearse been concerned to build up a body of teachers committed not only to the cultural aspirations of St Enda's but also to it as a site for learning, then the school might have fared better in the lean years of the 1920s and 1930s'.[49]

After Pearse's execution, the standard of education undoubtedly dropped and the range of subjects on offer in the curriculum was significantly reduced. The few references to St Enda's in contemporary newspapers were never in the context of academic or sporting achievements. When the school was mentioned it was invariably in connection with the attendance of the boys (and past pupils) at anniversary masses for Patrick and Willie or at the annual ceremonies to commemorate the 1916 Rising or other special occasions, such as in September 1931, when Margaret brought forty-two school boys to the offices of the *Irish Press* for a tour of its various departments and machinery.[50] In the post-1916 period, one could argue that the school was less important as an educational centre and more significant as a safe and supportive environment for the children of those who were involved in the Rising.

A letter received by the authors from past pupil and centenarian, Fr Joseph Mallin, son of executed leader Michael

Mallin, suggests that Margaret and her mother were unstintingly loyal to the families of those connected with the Rising; perhaps they regarded the provision of education through St Enda's as yet another means of supporting these families. Fr Mallin wrote:

> I knew Miss Margaret Pearse very well. She taught Religious Instruction and French. She was very steady and could control the boys well in class. She was firm and did not approve of bad behaviour. Our family owes her a debt of gratitude … It was she who arranged to take my younger sister, then almost eight years and me to St Enda's. Miss Pearse arranged schooling for my sister at the Loreto School, Rathfarnham and she instructed her for First Holy Communion. She also arranged a helper for my mother in 1947–48 when my mother was laid up. Our family was not unique, they helped so many others in similar circumstances. [51]

The closure of St Enda's in 1935 officially marked the end of Patrick's and the Pearse family's pedagogical experiment.

CHAPTER 5

Mary Brigid: Literature, Loss and Litigation

> You are cordially invited to a musical soirée at the residence
> of Mary Brigid Pearse ... any mention of politics will result
> in removal by Civic Guard.[1]
>
> Mary Brigid Pearse

After her brothers' executions, Mary Brigid chose to remain out of public and political life. As her mother and sister were increasingly burdened with the legacy of Patrick and Willie, Mary Brigid focused on teaching music and writing at her home in 20 Ashfield Park, Terenure, and later in 6 Beaufort Villas, Rathfarnham. Prior to the Rising, Mary Brigid's literary compositions were primarily one-act original dramas or adaptations of novellas by Charles Dickens for the Leinster Stage Society. In October 1916, one of her short stories, 'An Sagart', which told the story of two boys dressing up and re-enactng the mass in their home, was pirated from *The Cross* magazine and published by the Cork Free Press.[2] The editor of *The Cross*, a publication of the Passonist Order, was understandably furious but the act was indicative of the increasing public interest in the Pearse family in the immediate aftermath of the Rising. Mary Brigid's literary successes were always linked with Patrick. Her first major work, *The Murphys of*

Ballystack, was published in 1917 by M.H. Gill & Son, who had published lectures by Patrick in 1898. An advertisement for Mary Brigid's book in the *Irish Independent* in July 1917 simply stated, 'Ready on Wednesday, *The Murphys of Ballystack* by Mary B. Pearse (Sister of the late P.H. Pearse).'[3]

The novel tells the story of the exploits of the Murphy family, who run the village shop in Ballystack, their wealthy neighbour Barney O'Hagan and his chauffeur, Miles, who spends his days concocting mischievous plans involving his beloved 'mothor car'. Murphy's business dealings are often dubious. His merchandise is invariably faulty and everything in the shop 'reeks' of cheap paraffin oil. Murphy has a reputation for selling toy crocodiles whose wheels come off; several children had been saved from choking on these by Dr Wilson, the village doctor. The Murphys live with their five children and an eccentric elderly aunt. Shaun, the eldest son, writes poetry and, in a bid to adopt an artistic persona, he 'sport[s] long hair and a preposterous tie'.[4] The author remarks that he had only recently discovered his literary talents, '[f]or quite suddenly Shaun had awoke to the fact that as well as being a poet, he was also a playwright. Unfortunately, however, none of the managers to whom he submitted his work, had awoken to the same fact.'[5] In an effort to sound more genteel, his sisters Brigid and Sarah change their names to Belinda and Sadie. When Belinda marries Donal O'Grady, a barrister with a house in Merrion Square, she succeeds in realising her parents' burning ambition of climbing the social ladder.

The novel, which runs to almost 250 pages, is best described as a series of short stories with common characters; consequently, the narrative is not as fully developed as one would expect in a novel. Although Ruth Dudley Edwards described the book as 'an excruciating piece of sub-Somerville and Ross, which reflected an urban mind's notion of rustic frolics',[6] Mary Brigid's work is a well-written, often humurous narrative of one family's attempt to improve its social status, and was generally well received. A reviewer in *The Tablet*, however, suggested that the book should have ended at Chapter Ten and the remaining chapters transformed into a separate novel about 'the gay, mischievous, most loveable' Barney O'Hagan.[7] Mary Brigid's first major literary success was to prove short-lived as she struggled over the next three decades to get work published. In the Pearse Archive in Kilmainham Gaol there are numerous rejection letters from various publishers in Ireland and England[8] and her agent, Donald N.G. Craig, based in Holycross, Co. Tipperary, even suggested that she should enrol in a course for short-story writing to improve her skills.[9]

With a cloud over her literary career, she increasingly relied on her musical competency and versatility as a multi-instrumentalist to derive a living from the 1920s onwards. In addition to her main instruments, piano and harp, she also offered lessons in violin, cello and mandolin at her home in Terenure as well as teaching music at St Enda's. She also arranged a number of Irish airs for voice and piano, and voice with harp accompaniment; these included 'Oró Sé do Bheatha Bhaile', 'An Spailpín Fánach', 'Cailín Deas Cruite na mBó', 'An Draighnean Donn', 'Cnocáinín Aerach Chill Mhuire', 'The Fairy Boy' and 'The Old Grey Mare'. Whether she used these arrangements to teach her students or intended to have them published in a collection is unclear, but they demonstrate her strong grasp of the rudiments of music and their application in the harmonisation and arrangement of melodies.

During the 1920s and early 1930s Mary Brigid spent much of her time writing short stories, plays, children's stories and articles (see Appendix 2). She also gave a number of radio interviews on Patrick's life. Although some plays, like *The King's Jester*, were written in three acts, her preferred genre was short one-act plays, such as *The Shamrock Girl* and *Luck*, a farce set in an Irish country kitchen. Many of her works were inspired by religious figures and/or themes e.g. *St Brigid's Procession* and *The Saint of Aran*, which was about St Enda's conversion to Christianity. She also wrote about the Eucharistic Congress in Dublin in 1932 in 'Some impressions of the Eucharistic Congress Week by a

Dubliner', but this was not published. Historical figures or events were the inspiration for plays such as *Brian Boru: A Historical Play in One Act* and *Triumph*. Only a one-act version of her play on Brian Ború is extant, though there is evidence to suggest that she intended to extend the narrative to produce a play in three acts.

She was most prolific in her composition of short stories and radio plays. *The Open Door*, which narrates the story of an Irish Christmas, was performed on Raidió Éireann and she adapted *Two Shots in the Dark*, which was originally written as a radio play, as a short story. She wrote over twenty short stories including 'Curtain Up', 'Lumen de Lumene', 'A Fantastic Fantasy', 'The Fairies Glen', 'The Pipe of Peace', 'A Spring Song', 'A Bank Holiday', 'The Lie', 'St Brigid's/The Shield', 'Some Un-seasonable Remarks', 'The Understudy' and 'Old Timsey's St Patrick's Pot'. There are also a number of incomplete stories, such as 'Foolish Fun'. She commenced two other novels, *Curly and the Persian* (see Appendix 4) and *The Romance of Castle Bawn*. The former, which followed the adventures of Curly the dog and Fluffs the cat, is one of many stories that reflected Mary Brigid's love of animals. Neither of these novels was published but an edited version of *The Romance of Castle Bawn* appeared in the *Irish Catholic* newspaper between April and October 1931.

Mary Brigid's best-known literary work is *The Home-Life of Pádraig Pearse, as told by himself his family and friends*, published in 1934. Its journey from inception to final publication was a long and difficult one that lasted over a decade. For many years, Mary Brigid's mother had urged her to write the story of Patrick's life; in fact it was Mrs Pearse who encouraged and supported Mary Brigid in her literary pursuits from a young age. When the editor of the Christian Brothers' magazine, *Our Boys*, asked her to contribute a series of articles on her brother, Mary Brigid happily obliged. The series, *The Life of Pádraig Pearse*, published in 1926, marked the tenth anniversary of the Rising.[10] The magazine, known for its frequent publication of articles on historic Irish figures, was an ideal medium for promoting Mary Brigid's work, and the serialisation proved very successful. Her mother and sister supported the endeavour and contributed their reminiscences to the project. Following this successful serialisation, Mary Brigid struggled to find a publisher for a book-length version of it. These were turbulent years for her, marked by the death of her mother and a bitter dispute with her sister.

Mrs Pearse had suffered from failing sight in later life, but her death on 22 April 1932 was unexpected. A few weeks before, she had attended a number of events in honour of Patrick and Willie. On 2 April, she and Margaret were honorary guests at the second annual reunion of Clann Éanna (St Enda's Past Pupils' Union) at the Gresham Hotel. At school gatherings and commemorative events, when Mrs Pearse spoke, it was invariably to recount the story of her last moments with Patrick and Willie. On that occasion, one of her last public appearances, she described the parting from her sons as 'one of the most precious and intimate memories of her life'.[11] After only a few days' illness, she died from erysipelas (a bacterial infection of the skin) aggravated by a weak heart. Shortly before her death, Margaret read an article to her mother about the previous day's proceedings in Dáil Éireann, which greatly amused her; a few moments later she received final absolution from Fr Mellett, a teacher at St Enda's, and died in the presence of Margaret and her nurse. Mary Brigid was not present.

The death of Mrs Pearse was widely reported in the media. Her daughter Margaret was mentioned as the chief mourner but Mary Brigid's name was omitted from several articles reporting on the funeral; she was also not mentioned in some subsequent reports of anniversary masses for her mother.[12] Tributes that appeared in various newspapers invariably commented on her gentle character and stoicism. They remarked on the sacrifice of her two sons so that Ireland could achieve its freedom from Britain. A journalist from the *Irish Independent* wrote:

> Few mothers have been called upon to make such a
> sacrifice for their country, and no one could have made it

more uncomplainingly ... she was a quiet, gentle lady with kindly, gracious manners, distinguished by her mass of beautiful white hair, fine features, and the complexion of a young girl. She was the worthy mother of such illustrious sons.[13]

Repeatedly, journalists employed stock phrases and clichéd language to highlight her family's sacrifice and to align her suffering with that of Mary's at the foot of the cross on Calvary:

In her, the womanhood of Ireland was enshrined – that great womanhood which has preserved for the Irish nation its heritage of nationality and its heritage of faith. For it was the women of this nation, who like the great women of Galilee, stood closest to the Cross and saw their sons die for truth. The instinct of a mother's protection for her children is the deepest of all human instincts, but to these women of our land there was a deeper impulse still; to rear sons who would go out and give their lives for the good of their nation.[14]

The representation of Mrs Pearse as the archetypal selfless Irish mother and the alignment of her patriotic and Christian sacrifice had its origin in this period, and this understanding of her, which was so widely espoused in contemporary newspapers, dominated any discussion of Patrick and his family in the following decades.

Although Mrs Pearse had requested a private funeral, the Fianna Fáil National Executive, of which Margaret was a member, insisted that the Irish people would expect a public funeral and some state involvement. Margaret acquiesced to their request. Mrs Pearse was laid out in St Enda's chapel and thousands of people came to the school on 24 April to pay their respects. Her requiem mass took place on 26 April at the Church of the Annunciation, Rathfarnham, and was celebrated by Fr T. MacNevin, parish priest, and concelebrated by Fr Joseph Valentine,

Fr Laurence Kelly and Fr Joseph Erraughty SJ, with music provided by the Jesuit choir from Rathfarnham Castle, conducted by Fr Kevin Smyth. The funeral was attended by people from across the political spectrum but, unsurprisingly, Fianna Fáil (the Government party) who took charge of the proceedings, were most prominent during the period of mourning. Fianna Fáil used the funeral of Mrs Pearse to reassert publicly their republican lineage and their claim to the inheritance of the ideals of 1916.

After the mass, Mrs Pearse's remains were brought to City Hall for the lying-in-state where an estimated 40,000 people paid their respects.[15] From City Hall, the funeral cortège made its way through the main streets of the city, briefly pausing at the GPO. A procession of 15,000 people followed the coffin to Glasnevin Cemetery, including past and present pupils and staff of St Enda's, the Fintan Lalor Pipers' Band, The O'Rahilly Band, St James's Band, approximately sixty priests, over a thousand members of Fianna Fáil, representatives from various Corporations and County Councils from around Ireland, members of the GAA, Gaelic League, Irish Republican Soldiers' Federation, Dublin Brigade of the Old IRA and the Catholic Girl Guides. Éamon de Valera delivered the graveside oration, praising Mrs Pearse for her courage in upholding her sons' ideals:

> But for the fame of her sons[,] the noble woman at whose grave we are gathered would, perhaps, never have been known outside a narrow circle of personal friends ... Since she parted with Padraic and Willie on Easter Monday, 1916, her task, in her own words, has been to 'hold what they upheld'. She fulfilled it to the end, without bitterness in bitter years, without complaint when the cause that her sons had died for seemed all but hopeless. Her courage, her charity, her cheerfulness during those years have been an inspiration to all who have had the privilege of her friendship ... The memory of her life remains with us, however, a source of strength in the work that lies ahead,

the work of realising the ideal for which she suffered and her sons gave their lives – an Ireland 'not free merely but Gaelic as well, not Gaelic merely but free as well'.[16]

De Valera's words must have rung hollow for Margaret particularly in light of his lack of financial support for St Enda's. However, Margaret was dignified and unstinting in her support of her mother's friend and her endorsement of de Valera as successor to the ideals of her brother Patrick.

According to Mrs Pearse's will, which was made on 20 April 1932, Margaret was appointed sole executrix. Because the will was made only days before her death, it was not legally binding; consequently, Margaret was not obliged to abide by its terms. Nevertheless, Margaret was happy to discharge her duty as executrix. Mrs Pearse's estate was valued at £1,586. St Enda's was left to her daughter Margaret for the duration of her life; to be gifted, on her death, to the Irish State, as a memorial to Patrick and Willie. Mrs Pearse specified that St Enda's and its grounds were not to be used as a school or institution and that its furniture was to remain there until Margaret's death, unless her niece, Mary Kate Shovelton, wished to select certain objects.[17] Cullenswood House was bequeathed jointly to Margaret and Mary Brigid, and after their deaths, the proceeds of the sale of the property were to be used to fund future anniversary masses for Mrs Pearse and deceased members of her family. Number 20 Ashfield Park and its furniture was left to Mary Brigid; upon her death, the property was to pass to Lillian Byrne, a carer/companion of Mary Brigid, on whose own death the house was to be sold and proceeds used to pay minor legacies.

The will stipulated that Mary Byrne, a family friend, was to receive the rent from two bungalows on the grounds of St Enda's during her lifetime and dividends from Mrs Pearse's shares; on Byrne's death, these shares would revert to Mary Brigid, Margaret and their cousin, Margaret Brady. If Margaret (Pearse) predeceased Margaret Brady, however, the shares were to be sold and proceeds

Pearse children. Left to right: Willie, Patrick, Margaret and Mary Brigid.
(Courtesy of PMSTE/OPW)

Margaret Pearse aged fifteen.
(Courtesy of the Holy Faith Sisters
Congregational Archives, Glasnevin)

Mary Brigid and Willie Pearse and their cousin John Kelly. (Courtesy of PMSTE/OPW)

Mary Brigid Pearse. (Courtesy of PMSTE/OPW)

LEINSTER STAGE ··· SOCIETY ·

Programme.
Friday, May, 27th, 1910,
at 8.15.

Abbey Theatre.

Programme for the Leinster Stage Society performance at the Abbey Theatre on 27 May 1910. (Courtesy of PMSTE/OPW)

The Message:

A Play in One Act and an Epilogue.

By M. B. PEARSE.

Donal	-	WILLIAM PEARSE.
Shaun	-	FRED. HOLDEN.
Tadhg.	-	MORGAN O'FRIEL.
A Neighbour	-	J. DORAN.
Maire	-	MISS JULIE HAYDEN.
Noreen	-	MAUREEN NUGENT.
Cathleen	-	MISS ELLA DELANEY.
Lady Rivers	-	MISS M. ANDERSON.
Mona Fitzgerald	-	MISS MARY FITZGERALD.

SCENE :—Maire's Kitchen.

Evening.—The Departure of the Swallows.

EPILOGUE :

Following Year.—The Return of the Swallows.

The Countess of Strasbourg:

An Incident of 1805

BY A. McGLOUGHLIN.

Napoleon	-	WILLIAM PEARSE.
Marshal Ney	-	EAMONN BULFIN.
General Klenau (of the Austrian Army)	SORLEY MACGARVEY.
Pierre (an Innkeeper)	-	FRED. A. McDONALD.
Captain Bernard	-	RICHARD BOYD.
Mdlle. Renée Mayenne (a Vivandière)	MISS MARY FITZGERALD.

SCENE :—Interior of an Inn on the outskirts of Ulm.

Time.—Evening, October 5th, 1805.

"The close of the Austrian Campaign witnessed the advance of a very capable man." *Bourrienne's Memoirs of Napoleon.*

Over the Stile:

A Play in Two Scenes,

BY M. B. PEARSE.

Pat Casey	-	FRED. A. McDONALD.
Barney O'Brien } Field hands }	WILLIAM PEARSE.
Alec, a Scotchman }	MORGAN O'FRIEL.
Mrs. Casey	-	MISS JULIE HAYDEN.
Katie	-	MISS ELLEN DELANEY.
Peggy	-	MISS MARY FITZGERALD.

SCENE I.—Exterior of Pat Casey's Cottage.

By the Stile.—Sunset.

SCENE II.—Over the Stile—At the Well.

Next Evening.

The Transformation of Fionn,

BY STANDISH O'GRADY.

Fionn	-	WILLIAM PEARSE.
Nod	-	RICHARD BOYD.
Ossian	-	MORGAN O'FRIEL.
Fairy	-	MISS MARY FITZGERALD.

Warriors and Gillies :—EAMONN BULFIN, SORLEY MACGARVEY, FRED. HOLDEN, TADHG. CARLETON.

SCENE : —By the Lake on Slieve Gullion.

Original Music by Tomás MacDonnchill.

During the Intervals the String Orchestra will play :—

1.	Irish Airs	-	Volti.
2.	Tannhauser	-	Wagner.
3.		Selected.	
4.	Gavotte	Selected.	

ANTIQUES LENT BY MESSRS. WALSH.

NEXT WEEK—
Dublin Art Students' Union in Five Plays.

Programme for the Leinster Stage Society performance at the Abbey Theatre on 27 May 1910. (Courtesy of PMSTE/OPW)

Margaret Pearse and her niece Florence. Margaret was a witness at Florence's wedding to William Scarlett in 1915. (Courtesy of PMSTE/OPW)

Mrs Pearse and Joseph Mallin. (Courtesy of PMSTE/OPW)

Margaret Pearse. (Courtesy of PMSTE/OPW)

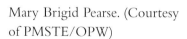
Mary Brigid Pearse. (Courtesy of PMSTE/OPW)

Mary Brigid Pearse's drawing of Ceola, her beloved dog. (Courtesy of PMSTE/OPW)

Left to right: Fr Joseph Smith, Mrs Pearse, Margaret Pearse and Fr Eugene Nevin on the steps of St Enda's. (Courtesy of the Archive of the Passionist Community, Mount Argus)

Senator Margaret Pearse by Robert
Pyke. (Private Collection)

Margaret Pearse at Áras an Uachtaráin. (Courtesy of
PMSTE/OPW)

IRISH PRESS PHOTO

Margaret Pearse and Éamon de Valera at Arbour Hill, Dublin. (Courtesy of PMSTE/OPW)

Margaret Pearse and Éamon de Valera at the Linden Convalescent Home, Blackrock, Co. Dublin. (Courtesy of PMSTE/OPW)

used to fund scholarships for students attending Irish-speaking schools in Connemara. Mrs Pearse left her shares in the *Irish Press* to her daughter Margaret. She also bequeathed money, in equal share, to the Carmelite Fathers of Whitefriar Street, the Jesuit Fathers of Rathfarnham and the Passionist Fathers of Mount Argus, Dublin.

Soon after the terms of Mrs Pearse's will were disclosed, Mary Brigid sought legal advice. She engaged the services of Meldon Solicitors of 9 Bachelor's Walk, Dublin in the summer of 1933 and nominated Lilian Byrne to negotiate on her behalf. Mary Brigid was unhappy with the terms of the will and Margaret's appointment as executrix. The relationship between the two sisters had been fractious since their childhood, and Patrick or their mother often acted as peacemaker between them. The Pearse Archive in Kilmainham Gaol contains postcards and objects revealing that the sisters occasionally set aside their differences. On Margaret's twentieth birthday, Mary Brigid gave her a book, *The Angel of the Altar: or, the Love of the Most Adorable and Most Sacred Heart of Jesus*, with the inscription 'To dear Maggie, Wishing her a happy birthday and a great many of them. From her loving and grateful sister Mimmy.'[18] In 1931, Margaret went to considerable effort to find a suitable companion/carer for Mary Brigid. Despite these occasional examples of positive relations between them, it seems that whatever relationship existed before their mother's death was irrevocably destroyed following the reading of her will.

Prior to 1933, Mary Brigid expressed no interest in her family's finances; her family had always provided for her and she had no financial concerns. When Patrick died, his debts passed to his mother and then to Margaret. At the time of her death, Mrs Pearse's debt was £425.8s.7d. and to cover the debt, Margaret sold the Corporation shares which had been left to her by her mother. Mary Brigid was furious that the bank had permitted Margaret to sell off the stock and she was particularly indignant that the proceeds of the sale were being used to pay off their mother's debt without her permission. Margaret explained that, even after the sale of the Corporation shares, there was an outstanding debt of £85 and additional bank debt, so she suggested selling 20 Ashfield Park, where Mary Brigid resided. Mary Brigid was not liable for any of these debts but her solicitor informed her that, if there was a shortfall of assets, some property or other assets would have to be sold to cover the debt.

Through her solicitors, Mary Brigid demanded that Margaret's solicitor, Daniel C. Maher of 20 Westland Row, provide a valuation of each of the properties at The Hermitage, Cullenswood House and 20 Ashfield Park, and a detailed statement of their mother's stocks and shares. In February 1934, Mary Brigid dismissed her solicitors and engaged her neighbour, Bernard Bernstein, a solicitor working at City Chambers, 69–70 Dame Street. Bernstein wrote to Margaret's solicitors requesting a statement of royalties from Patrick's literary works, details of the cottage in Rosmuc, and a statement of the rents collected from, and outgoings of, the various properties since their mother's death.[19] On 19 April 1934, Bernstein informed Margaret, through her solicitor, that Mary Brigid wanted all legal and financial matters to be resolved immediately so that they would have no further reason to communicate with each other.[20]

Margaret was slow to provide Bernstein with a detailed statement of the rents from the various properties. She feared that, if Mary Brigid took charge of collecting her share of the rental income, the tenants would become suspicious and might learn of the ongoing disagreements between the sisters. Margaret dreaded the prospect of the Pearse name receiving negative press. Letters between the solicitors of Margaret and Mary Brigid show that Mary Brigid was becoming increasingly frustrated with the situation. Bernstein (on Mary Brigid's behalf) wrote:

> [i]t is your client who is embarrassing and annoying my client ... It is also important for my clients to know the full names and addresses of Joyce and Burke and of the

Cullenswood tenants. I can assure you that this question is not a trivial one … The information is sought by persons who are entitled to know. You did not make any reference at all to the rents received by your client for the quarter ended 20th March last and which your client actually got. I wonder did your client think it right to delay remittances when she actually got the cash. Please therefore get her to send on my client's moiety at once. There is no reason whatsoever why my client should not get her half-share the moment your client receives the rent.[21]

Mary Brigid was convinced that her sister was misappropriating her inheritance. She demanded the deeds to 20 Ashfield Park, the house bequeathed to her for her lifetime, and insisted that Margaret purchase her half-share in Cullenswood House. Mary Brigid was not given the deeds and they were held in trust by Margaret's solicitors. In any case, it was not commonplace for women to be given deeds at this time and, as the house was left to her to reside in for her lifetime, there was no legal reason for her to have them. Cullenswood House was already mortgaged and, according to the terms of their mother's will, could not be sold until after their deaths. Margaret had already paid the rates of £30.18s.1d. on the property for the period 1933–34 and claimed that Mary Brigid had not paid her half-share; there was also a sum of £55.19s.8d. outstanding on the property of which Mary Brigid owed half.

Mary Brigid, who was becoming progressively more desperate to gain the upper hand against Margaret, wrote to Anna Smith, who had accompanied her mother on her USA tour in 1924, requesting a statement of the income derived from the trip. No statement was forthcoming as Smith had not kept records from a trip which had taken place over ten years before. In April 1934, Mary Brigid expressed a desire for her solicitor to instigate legal proceedings against her sister, but Bernstein warned against this. With threats of legal action against her, Margaret approached

Éamon de Valera, who suggested that the dispute might be resolved through arbitration; however, this option was not pursued.

Relations between the sisters further deteriorated with the publication of *The Home-Life of Pádraig Pearse* in late 1934. Because sections of Patrick's unfinished autobiography were incorporated into the book, both Margaret and Mary Brigid were entitled to royalties from the publication. Margaret wrote to Mary Brigid's publisher, Browne and Nolan, to inform them that she had not consented to the publication and was due a share of the royalties.[22] Mary Brigid disputed Margaret's claim and, soon after, Margaret relinquished her rights to the royalties. Mary Brigid resented her sister's actions and immediately contacted the publishers to cancel the print run. Browne and Nolan, having invested £138.19s.6d. in printing five hundred copies, were reluctant to agree to her demands.

Nonetheless, Mary Brigid insisted that she would prefer to repay personally the amount of their investment to date rather than have any doubt about the ownership of the manuscript. All books were subsequently withdrawn and Mary Brigid purchased all unsold copies. Later Mary Brigid, with the help of Kathleen Cruise O'Brien, approached Eason & Sons with a view to selling the remainder of her stock. Easons agreed to sell the book on condition that Mary Brigid would explain 'the circumstance which interefered with its distribution' and provide a written guarantee that all issues had been satisfactorily resolved.[23] Robert Eason was ultimately reassured and a few weeks later agreed to purchase approximately four hundred copies at 1/6d. per copy.[24]

Mary Brigid frequently confided in her friends about the difficulties she was experiencing with Margaret. Fr Joseph Smith, based in Lancashire, expressed his sadness at hearing of Margaret's 'truculent attitude' towards her sister and advised Mary Brigid to be reasonable, advice which unfortunately she did not heed. He said:

> I cannot understand anyone being so implacable, without any necessity and against a sister. But try not to be so upset about it and above all don't try to stop the book. It will do

you much good indirectly, and bring you an increase of reputation ... The ms [manuscript] of Patrick's autobiography may be her property now – but it was Mrs Pearse's once, and while it was Mrs Pearse's, Mrs Pearse gave you permission to use it ... Don't mind what Maggie says: she is probably trying to bluff or bully you. Leave things in the solicitor's hands, and don't write letters to B&N [Browne and Nolan].[25]

In correspondence with Fr Joseph, Mary Brigid also mentioned her disappointment that the publishers insisted on using her initials M.B. instead of her full name. She felt this was degrading and that they were only interested in publishing her book because of the Pearse surname. Mary Brigid was undoubtedly correct as the publishers were cognisant that the biggest attraction and potential selling point of the book was that Mary Brigid and Patrick were siblings.

It seems that the publication of the book was not the only contentious issue between Margaret and Mary Brigid at this time. The royalties from Patrick's literary works were divided in the ratio of two-thirds to Margaret and one-third to Mary Brigid. These were paid directly to Margaret by publishers such as the Educational Company, Talbot Press and Folens, and she subsequently paid Mary Brigid. The irregularity of the payments irked Mary Brigid and she contacted each of the publishers requesting that her share of the royalties be paid directly to her. Although Margaret initially refused Mary Brigid's demands, in mid-February 1935, she relented and instructed the Educational Company to pay Mary Brigid's share of the royalties directly to her. Similar arrangements were agreed with other publishers during the following months.

By the end of 1935, Mary Brigid's main grievances over property, rental income and the royalties from Patrick's literary works and *The Home-Life* had been resolved, but she was still not satisfied. Despite legal advice to the contrary, she decided to pursue a case against her sister through the courts on the grounds of the maladministration of her mother's will. In September 1935, contemporary newspapers such as the *Irish Examiner* and *Evening Herald* featured short articles entitled 'Sisters at Law' and 'Sisters' Dispute', which informed the reader that the case was being adjourned until 7 October 1935.[26] There were no further reports or references to the action in newspapers in the following months. Her relationship with her solicitor Bernard Bernstein became increasingly strained in this period. In a letter dated 12 November 1935, he wrote:

> I want you to be so careful about your case that everything I do for you should be straight, honest and above board. You should not blame Counsel. You and they simply cannot see eye to eye. That is all there is to it. I have been a good friend to you from the day I undertook your affairs. If you want me to retire from the case then I will do so. I have done everything possible for you both as your lawyer and as your friend but I do not appear to be appreciated.[27]

Mary Brigid's erratic behaviour and her unwillingness to accept the advice of her legal counsel embarrassed and irritated Bernstein. He informed her:

> Your case is not worrying me. It is yourself who worries me. Why could you not leave me alone and stop harrying me? If you do not want me to go on with your case then I will do so. But I will say this ... so far as Counsel and I are concerned we have done our utmost to get you to settle on terms which to us cover and protect your interests amply, and if you want to throw away your money on costs then you can do so.[28]

In May 1936, Mary Brigid discharged her Senior and Junior Counsel (Messrs Lavery and Hare). Shortly afterwards, she settled her bill of *c.£*140 with Bernstein and had no further contact with him. In her final letter to Bernstein she wrote, 'I have dismissed Mr Lavery and Mr Hare, and have no intention of re-engaging them ever again. Is not this statement sufficiently explicit for them, and you? Please show the gentlemen (who have both let me down callously when I was depending on them) this letter, so that there can be no confusion or misunderstanding on this matter anymore!'[29]

The publication of *The Home-Life of Pádraig Pearse* was completely overshadowed by the falling out between Mary Brigid and her sister. Margaret and her mother had supported Mary Brigid's literary project by contributing written accounts of Patrick and the resulting publication should have been an important celebration in the lives of the Pearse family. Unfortunately, it was not. Mary Brigid's narrative of the family's idyllic childhood was a stark contrast to the acrimonious dispute between the sisters in adulthood; it was also a reminder of the importance of Patrick and his mother as unifying figures within the Pearse family.

The Home-Life of Pádraig Pearse is one of the most significant books written on Patrick and an important source for biographers. Quite simply, it humanises Patrick in a way that no other book has ever done. The author, being the subject's sister, adds an intimacy and warmth to the narrative of the book which would not be possible by another author. In its introduction, Browne and Nolan stressed the unique content of the book and its 'unconventional' yet highly significant 'intimate view' of Patrick's childhood and early adulthood.[30] The publishers referenced the events of Easter 1916, but only to contrast the pathos of Patrick's death with the happiness and contentment of his early life:

> Everyone must be touched by the poignant contrast between the care-free gaiety of those sunny days and the story of struggle and sacrifice and the final tragedy which later years were to bring. On that night when Pearse sat

alone in his cell at Kilmainham awaiting the fatal dawn, his thoughts, as we know, wandered back with love and yearning to the old home and its inmates.[31]

The first part of the book incorporates five chapters of Patrick's unfinished autobiography. It is unclear when Patrick wrote this material, but his objective was to record what he had done, 'not to explain, or to apologise for, or to justify anything'.[32] Consequently, the information is presented in a factual and unemotional manner. He was impatient about failures in his life that he blamed on an inability to live in the moment; he believed that 'the remembered or imagined experience [was] more insistent than the actual'.[33] In the second part of *The Home-Life*, Mary Brigid recalls her memories of growing up in the Pearse home and shares some recollections of Patrick by his mother and sister. The book concludes with contributions from relations, friends and former students on Patrick's character and his vocation as a teacher.

Part One (Patrick's autobiography), which begins with a chapter entitled 'Myself-My Father-My Mother and her People', presents a recurring theme of the book, namely the happiness that Margaret, Willie, Patrick and Mary Brigid enjoyed in childhood. Patrick wrote, 'continually my thoughts have gone back to the places that were first familiar to me, and my ear has heard the voices that it first heard'[34] and stated that '[t]wo things have constantly pulled at cross-purposes in me: one, a deep homing instinct, a desire beyond words to be at home always, with the same beloved faces, the same familiar shapes and sounds about me; the other, an impulse to seek hard things to do, to go on far quests and fight for lost causes'.[35] Although Patrick mentions Margaret and Mary Brigid, the strong devotion to his brother and companion Willie dominates the autobiographical section: '[a]s a boy he was my only playmate; as a man he has been my only intimate friend. We have done and suffered much together, and we have shared together a few deep joys.'[36] Part One ends abruptly with Patrick philosophising about how a potentially fatal childhood illness shaped his character and strengthened his resolve in adulthood.

Many members of the Pearse family provided Mary Brigid with their reminiscences of Patrick or contributed written accounts for inclusion in the book. Mrs Pearse's contribution was a six-page piece entitled 'A Mother's Golden Memories' in which she recalled Patrick's kindness to Mary Brigid and his devotion to his brother. She hoped that her brief personal account of Patrick's childhood would inspire and impress upon young people that they too could 'grow up as this gentle teacher and lover of children grew up – affectionate, kindly, and brave, as he was in his childhood days'.[37] In Margaret's piece, 'A Few Traits in the Character of Pádraig Pearse', she highlighted Patrick's nationalism and piety. Margaret's emphasis on the political and religous aspects of Patrick's character is in strong contrast to Mary Brigid's more personal and affectionate account of her brother. The Pearse's half-sister, Emily Pearse McGloughlin, wrote a few paragraphs on Patrick's role as a page at her wedding. She commented that she could hardly have imagined on her wedding day 'the power that my small, velvet-clad page was to hold some day in his frail-looking tiny person!'[38] Emily's son, Alfred, remembered Patrick's love of practical jokes and jokers. He cited one occasion when Patrick wandered around Connemara dressed as a tramp.

The final section of *The Home-Life* includes correspondence from relations, friends and colleagues. Edward O'Neill, a schoolmate from the CBS, recalled a very reserved schoolboy and voracious reader; a member of football and boxing clubs who once knocked out a boy who mocked him for missing a kick on the football pitch. O'Neill mentioned that Patrick loved Irish literature and debating and that he was destined to have 'no ordinary life'.[39] Mrs Máire Connolly of Connemara, whose son was educated at St Enda's, fondly remembered Patrick's visits to her home in Connemara, his simplicity and his love of children, animals and nature. Frank O'Nolan, a teacher at St Enda's, described the respect and admiration Patrick's students had for him. He also related an entertaining incident when a policeman called to St Enda's to serve a summons on him to appear in Green Street Court for cycling his bicycle after dark without a light. When O'Nolan refused to leave his classroom, the policeman spoke to Patrick, who assured him that, as an officer of the High Court, he would serve the summons on O'Nolan himself.

Perhaps the person most in awe of Patrick Pearse was Mary Brigid. One could argue that a weakness of the book is Mary Brigid's lack of objectivity about her brother Patrick. In light of the kindness he had shown her during his life, the book was unlikely to ever have been anything other than her homage to a lost and much-loved brother. Every sentence in the book was carefully constructed, and every recollection, story and correspondence was carefully chosen. She even omitted some sections from the original manuscript of Patrick's autobiography, particularly those referring to the family's humble origins. This was undoubtedly due to her pride but also because Mary Brigid was adamant that nothing, not even her family's financial history or social status, would impinge on the story of her brother. He was presented as a boy who adored his family and was adored by them. Mary Brigid acknowledged his intelligence, piety, strong communication and leadership skills, but also spoke about his generosity, sense of humour, roguish nature, his devotion to his family and his fondness for nuts, almonds, coconuts, a stick of barley or Turkish delight.

Although the book concludes with Patrick's farewell letter to his mother and sisters from Kilmainham Gaol, there are few references in *The Home-Life* to his politics, the Rising or his execution. This is really a book about the close bond Mary Brigid and Patrick enjoyed as children, their shared shyness and reserve, and her admiration for his gentleness and humour. The following paragraph affectionately captured this:

> I can see, as in a glass, this gentle boy-priest in many different phases of his life. I can see him as a small laddie,

serene-eyed and happy-hearted – though always rather quiet – hurrying to school, the 'little brother of his heart' trotting beside him, for the two were never apart. I can see him as an earnest student toiling unceasingly in preparation for examinations, and winning many fine laurels. I can see him in his young manhood, a little less dreamy than when he was a boy, but still with his broad white brows bent over his books; still climbing the ladder which leads to fame. But although all these visions are as clear to me as is the shining of crystals in dark places, there is one vision more vivid than all the rest – that tender vision of the innocent little '*sagart*' standing before the homely altar in the sunny room of the old house in Brunswick Street. I can see his little outstretched hands and earnest boyish face. I can even hear his young voice whispering reverently '*Ite, missa est.*'[40]

The Home-Life received generally positive reviews and was praised for the insight it provided into 'the ideals that formed themselves so definitely in [Patrick's] young manhood'.[41] It is noteworthy that reviews of the reprinted book in 1979 were less favourable and perhaps reflected the change in attitude to the legacy of Patrick Pearse and the increasing tendency to question the prevailing nationalist interpretation of the Rising in this period.

Mary Brigid continued to write and teach music throughout the 1930s and 1940s and gave several broadcasts on the life of her brother, but unfortunately these are not extant. She was in regular correspondence with relatives and friends, in particular her cousin, Mary Kate Shovelton and her friend, Fr Francis Farrell, who was based in Tanganyika (now Tanzania). Her state of health seemed to be a recurring theme in her correspondence. In 1936 Fr Farrell wrote: 'I do hope your health has improved, or that at least you have learned how one can be very happy in the midst of suffering. I know what a hard time you have, but I know too that it only increases suffering when one resents it and tries to fight against it. One can always "make the best of things, even a bad lot".'[42]

Unfortunately, Mary Brigid's health did not improve. She suffered from high blood pressure and neurosis and died, aged sixty-three, on 12 November 1947, of myocardial degeneration and hypertension at her home in Beaufort Villas. Her requiem mass took place on Saturday, 15 November at the Church of the Annunciation. The chief celebrant was Fr Joseph Mallin SJ, a former student of St Enda's and harp student of Mary Brigid's. He was joined by several past pupils of the school, who carried her coffin from the church. Over twenty priests, from religious orders such as the Jesuits, Carmelites, Passionists and Spiritans, concelebrated the mass. Among the large congregation were President Seán T. O'Kelly, Taoiseach Éamon de Valera, Attorney General Cearbhall Ó Dálaigh; government ministers, including Frank Aiken, Seán MacEntee, P.J. Little; members of the Dáil and Seanad, and senior military officials. The attendance of Joe O'Connor, representing the National Association of the Old IRA, Seán O'Moore (Chairman of the 1st Batallion of the Old IRA) and Kathleen Clarke, was indicative of the esteem in which the Pearse family was still held over three decades after the Rising.

Although Mary Brigid did not agree with her brothers' military activities and did not share 'in the political and social honours heaped on her mother and sister',[43] she was accorded the respect that membership of the Pearse family engendered. She was interred in Glasnevin Cemetery along with her mother and father. *The Home-Life* was later republished in 1979 to mark the centenary of Patrick's birth, but to date her other literary works have not been published. The few references to Mary Brigid since her death have been overwhelmingly negative; Ruth Dudley Edward's description of her as 'delicate, neurotic in later years, and a largely passive influence on Patrick', 'something of a hypochondriac, always needing a companion, financed by the family' and being 'an excitable woman, always swathed in coats in the hottest weather, while complaining incessantly of the heat' is indicative of this negativity.[44] She was a talented, formidable woman who suffered physically and psychologically throughout her life. In adulthood, she allowed Margaret to be the dutiful daughter while she focused on writing and other pursuits. She desired no responsibility but instead wanted to be carefree like a child and to be cared for and cosseted as she had been in Great Brunswick Street.

The Pearse Archive in Kilmainham Gaol contains numerous postcards on which Mary Brigid (in her twenties) painted animals (cats, dogs, etc.) and then sent the postcards pretending they were from 'Ceola' the dog. Perhaps it was this childishness or need for attention which most irked Margaret. In the many letters of condolence sent to Margaret following Mary Brigid's death, her suffering and hardship in life were recurring themes; '[s]he had a life of sore suffering, and I am sure she will now have her reward' wrote Fr Joseph; '[n]one of us knew the affliction which God willed to be hers' wrote Mary Murphy.[45] Most of those who sympathised with Margaret or congratulated her on her dedication to and support of Mary Brigid, were most likely unaware of the reality of the Pearse sister's relationship – a sororal relationship characterised by bitterness and jealousy.

CHAPTER 6

Margaret: The Politics of Being a Pearse

For those of us who had not the privilege of living through those stirring times, to have known Margaret Pearse was the next best thing.[1]

Unknown

When her mother died in 1932, Margaret Pearse assumed the role of matriarch, honouring the memory of her brothers at State and social events. She succeeded her mother on the Fianna Fáil National Executive and acted as co-treasurer and vice-president. From 1933 to 1937 she was a Fianna Fáil TD for County Dublin, the seat her mother held from 1921 to 1922. In an election campaign speech in 1933, Margaret appealed to her audience to continue to agitate for a united Ireland. She declared:

It is the same old fight ... the cause is the same, we have merely changed the tactics. We have the British on the one hand and Ireland and our hope for freedom on the other. There are many men here who were associated with my brothers in the days of the volunteers when you were preparing for 1916. You are now preparing for another fight and this time the way will be easier.[2]

Margaret was elected to the eighth Dáil, securing the final eighth seat in the constituency with 3,876 first-preference votes.[3] One of the first issues Margaret voted on was the removal of the Oath of Allegiance. Under the Anglo-Irish Treaty of 1921, TDs and senators were required to swear allegiance to the Constitution of the Irish Free State and to be faithful to the British sovereign. The Constitution (Removal of Oath) Act was passed on 3 May 1933, seventeen years to the day after Patrick's execution. Margaret later recalled that after the Act was passed, she went to Éamon de Valera's office to congratulate him and they were both overcome with tears.[4] Interestingly, de Valera had no desire to leave the Commonwealth at this point,[5] but, in contrast, Margaret was uncompromising in her desire for a united, autonomous Ireland.

On the campaign trail prior to the 1937 general election, Margaret highlighted the achievements of Fianna Fáil during its term in office and its commitment to the creation and expansion of industry. Eight hundred factories were built during the period 1933–7, resulting in increased employment throughout the country. She cited the expansion in the papermaking industry, with new plants at Clondalkin and Saggart, and an increase in the workforce from thirty in 1931, to 200 employees in 1937, as an example of Fianna Fáil's commitment to developing industry in her own constituency.[6] Margaret encouraged women to vote for her, promising that 'she would be the guardian of [their] … rights in the Dáil, if returned'.[7] She was, however, narrowly defeated in the 1937 general election, receiving 6,204 first-preference votes, a mere 208 votes behind Gerard McGowan (Labour), who won the fifth and final seat.[8] Margaret was particularly disappointed that she was not a member of the Dáil when the Constitution of Ireland (Bunreacht na hÉireann) was ratified in December 1937. Nonetheless, after losing in the election, she focused on gaining a seat in Seanad Éireann. Margaret was supported in her efforts by the *Irish Press* which wrote that

it was a cause of grief to her [Margaret's] friends and the
public when Miss Pearse was defeated for want of about
two hundred votes in the last General Election after
representing one of the Dublin constituencies since 1932.
Let us hope that success this time [in Seanad Éireann] will,
in some measure, atone for that disappointment.[9]

In 1938, Margaret was elected to the Administrative Panel of
Seanad Éireann. This Seanad only lasted a few months but
Margaret was re-elected to the Administrative Panel in the
election of August 1938, receiving almost twice the quota. She
was treasurer of the Irish branch of the Inter-Parliamentary
Union, an organisation founded in 1889 to prevent military
conflict by resolving disputes between certain European countries.
As a member of the Union, Margaret regularly attended
conferences abroad, including the thirty-fourth Inter-
Parliamentary Union Conference at The Hague from 22–27
August 1938. The conference, which took place at a momentous
time in European history, addressed the political state of Europe.
Margaret was defeated in the 1943 election to the Seanad, but
took her seat as a nominee of Taoiseach de Valera; he also
nominated her in 1944, 1951 and 1957. She was elected to the
Administrative Panel in 1948 and 1954. After the 1961 general
election, Margaret was one of eleven senators chosen by Taoiseach
Seán Lemass and he endorsed her again in 1965. She served as a
senator until her death in 1968.

Over the years, Margaret rarely spoke in the Dáil or Seanad;
however, in this respect, she was no different from many other
female TDs or Senators of the time. Female political appointments
were largely symbolic and reflected political parties' loyalties to
prominent Irish families. The surname Pearse was revered in
Fianna Fáil circles and Margaret Pearse became an emblematic
figurehead for the party, as her mother had been before her. She
appeared at Fianna Fáil's annual wreath laying commemorations
of 1916 at Arbour Hill for many years and often led with a decade

of the rosary in Irish. During the 1954 Seanad elections, a circular was issued appealing to members of the Administrative Panel for a first preference vote for Margaret as she was ill and unable to embark on the campaign trail: 'Miss Margaret Pearse is, rightly, held in the highest esteem by all Members of the Oireachtas because she has ever attended to her various duties with the most scrupulous devotion; but apart from that the sister of Pádraig and Willie Pearse, and sole survivor of the family residing at "St Enda's" is surely worthy of a tribute from every section of the Irish people.' [10]

Margaret spent over thirty years of her life as a politician and was the longest serving member of the Seanad at the time of her death. What appears on the surface to be an impressive poltical career was, in reality, relatively uneventful. She rarely contributed to debates in the Seanad during her long political life and her sole significant contribution concerned the Republic of Ireland Bill in 1948. The Bill proposed that Ireland become a republic, that the President of Ireland should have executive authority over any function of the state and that the State should cease to be a Dominion of the Crown. In debating the Bill, Margaret prefaced her speech by stating that she believed that Ireland had already been a Republic since the introduction of the 1937 Constitution; she had in fact previously described the Constitution as 'a declaration of independence'.[11] Her contribution, which is quoted in full below, was the only lengthy one she made during her political career in the Seanad.

> I want to say just a few words. First, there has been no confusion in my mind as to whether or not we had a republic. I know we have had it since 1937, but there has been confusion and it has been difficult sometimes to explain the position to other people, both within the country and outside it, to those who wish to see the truth and also to those who did not wish to see the truth, and there are none so blind as those who will not see. We all

know that the republic was first declared in 1916 outside the G.P.O., and it was approved by the people in 1918 and ratified by the Dáil in 1919. Through many vicissitudes and very sad years, it fought its way for life until 1923, when it was finally defeated in arms. Years passed, and another Government came in, and from the time that Government came in until 1937, bit by bit, to use a commonplace expression which I was accustomed to use at home amongst my friends, they made strenuous and successful efforts to dig us out of the Empire. One effort after the other succeeded, in face of fierce opposition. In 1937 we were in the position of having our republican Constitution and from that moment we were a republic.

Now the name is to be definitely affixed. There is much to rejoice about, because it is better to have the thing clear, especially when we can discuss it in a reasonable manner with other people, those who are with us and those who are against us. It has been a hard fight, and I am very pleased that this Government has been the Government to put the label on the republic, if you like to put it that way, to put the name on it. If the Fianna Fáil Government had attempted it – for wise and unwise reasons, they did not – it would not have gone through unanimously, and, in face of the world, it is a great thing to have such an important Bill as this going through unanimously.

There is one more thing I want to say, and it is a rather strange thing – I do not think there is one in the country who will agree with me – I am very sorry that we are not to be aliens. Why? Because we are aliens. I always like to be what I am. If I am rich, I do not want to be called poor, and, if I am poor, I do not want to be called rich. If I am Irish, I do not want to be called English, and, if I am English, I do not want to be called Irish. We are either Irish or

English, and, if we are Irish, we are aliens. I look on myself as an alien to England, as much as I am an alien to France, Italy, Germany, Switzerland or any other country.

It is not that I want to be an unfriendly alien – I am just as friendly as I am towards France – but I am definitely an alien to England, and I think it is an extraordinary thing that we are to be Irish and yet not aliens to England. It is trying to have the thing both ways and we cannot have it both ways. Perhaps we are still living another lie. However, I am very pleased to be here when this Bill is passing through, as I was very pleased and very proud, on 3rd May, 1933, to be one of 77 Deputies who voted to remove the Oath from the Constitution. That was the first big step and it was a proud and happy day when I went into the Division Lobby in the Dáil to vote against the detested Oath, which up to then all Deputies and Senators had to take.[12]

Aside from this contribution on the Republic of Ireland Bill, Margaret's other notable contributions were on a motion proposed by Senator Patrick Baxter seeking a higher fixed price for milk producers in 1943 and on the Adoption Bill (1952). During the debate on the Adoption Bill, Margaret voiced her concerns about the delay in passing the Bill. She observed that, because of this delay, certain children could not be adopted by families whom they had lived with and who wished to adopt them as they were over the age of seven, the legal limit for adoption. Other Senators suggested that an amendment should be introduced to deal with such cases, but that the age limit for adoption should not exceed seven years of age; the bill was passed with this amendment.

In contrast to her political contributions to the Dáil and Seanad, Margaret was outspoken on contemporary political, social and cultural issues in her public addresses, which she delivered around the country during the 1940s and 50s. Her politics were simple and transparent; she believed in a thirty-two-county republic with Irish as its first language. In June 1945, she delivered the opening address at the annual Aeridheacht (Fermanagh Feis) in Enniskillen, in which she urged her audience not to 'talk of "Northern Ireland" but of our separated Six Counties, our lost Six Counties that will be restored again soon'.[13]

Margaret was invited to speak at the Feis by nationalist politician Cahir Healy, who had also engaged her brother Patrick to speak at the Feis in 1906. Before her speech, the Tricolour was raised and 'Amhrán na bhFiann', the Irish national anthem, was played by a band from Omagh. She praised the organisers of the Feis for funding Irish language courses for local children and appealed to the younger members of her audience to speak Irish and to be nationalistic. She called for unity amongst religions on the island, declaring it 'stupid and ridiculous to make differences on account of religion'[14] and also used the opportunity to reiterate her views on partition:

> Don't think you are forgotten by us who are happily living in the Twenty-Six Counties. I assure you that you are not. We think of you frequently and consider is there any way we could help you out of this tremendous difficulty created by partition. We hope and pray that some of us – the older ones – may live to see the day of union, but definitely, the greater number of those here to-day will live to see it.[15]

A few years later, in February 1950, she again showed her support for anti-partition candidate Cahir Healy, by attending a rally in Coalisland, Co. Tyrone. Coalisland IRA veterans (with medals displayed) provided a bodyguard at the meeting, the Tricolour was hoisted on the platform, and the Irish national anthem was played by the Edendork Pipe Band. She addressed a crowd of a thousand and pleaded with them to exercise their franchise in support of Cahir Healy.[16] He was returned as an MP for Fermanagh and South Tyrone on 24 February 1950.

Margaret spoke regularly about two main issues at public gatherings, namely, partition and the promotion of the Irish language. In a speech to the Old IRA Literary and Debating Society at the Mansion House on 11 October 1950, she described partition as 'the greatest evil at present in this country'.[17] Her friend, Éamonn de Barra, noted that, throughout her long life, she availed of every opportunity to promote the language and to urge those with even a limited vocabulary to speak it, especially at home with children.[18] At a ceremony to mark her award of the Freedom of Wexford Borough in July 1952, and again at the opening of the Feis Maitiú in Dublin in May 1953, she emphasised the necessity of speaking Irish at home but also called for the preservation of traditional music and dance.[19] She vehemently opposed anyone who questioned the rightful place of Irish in the school curriculum, saying, 'I might suffer fools … but I will not tolerate traitors.'[20]

She believed that the future of the Irish language was dependant on the enthusiasm and willingness of young people to incorporate it into their daily activities. At an unveiling of a portrait of Patrick painted by Miss A. O'Connor (art specialist with the Civics Institute of Ireland playgrounds) at Pearse Square, Margaret urged young people to be proud of their city, to develop a sense of civic pride and to abstain from damaging property.[21] These ideals were undoubtedly influenced by Patrick; in the St Enda's school prospectus for 1908–9 it stated that staff was earnest in its 'efforts towards the awakening of a spirit of patriotism and the formation of a sense of civic and social duty'.[22] Some commentators have questioned Margaret's knowledge of and proficiency in the Irish language, with Ruth Dudley Edwards suggesting that it was limited to signing her name in Irish.[23] Although she was not as fluent in the language as Patrick, Willie or Mary Brigid, she achieved a certificate of Irish language competency in 1906/07 and could recite her prayers and the rosary in Irish.

After the death of her mother, Margaret became the public face of the Pearse family and represented the family at all commemorative events and political and social gatherings. She also bore the responsibility of protecting and preserving the legacy and reputations of her brothers. In August 1946, a number of letters written by Patrick before his death were presented to Margaret by John Donovan from London. These included some compositions and correspondence which were to be given to his mother, along with other personal effects, after his execution. The family claim that Patrick gave the items to Donovan's brother-in-law, Bernard Norton, a British army sergeant who worked in the records departments in Kilmainham 'as a token of his gratitude for the kindness he had shown him while imprisoned in Kilmainham Gaol'.[24]

Before Norton died in Leeds in 1922, he gave instructions that the items were to be returned to the Pearse family; this did not happen until 1946. On 23 September 1946, Margaret graciously treated Norton's widow, Christina Norton, her daughter, Joan Orange, and Joan's son, Anthony, to tea at Leinster House and afterwards posed for photographs on the steps of Leinster House. Amongst the documents which the Norton family gave to Margaret was a summary of Patrick's address at his court-martial which had hitherto been based only on eyewitness accounts.[25] Margaret subsequently presented these documents, which included a hand-written and typescript copy of Patrick's court-martial, to the Kilmainham Gaol Museum.[26]

Outside politics and cultural activism, Margaret spent much of her time corresponding with people from all over the world on a wide variety of topics. Much of the correspondence was concerned with royalties from Patrick's writings, performances of his works or enquiries from authors and publishers seeking permission to translate his works into different languages. Margaret, as her mother before her, received a constant stream of requests for tours of St Enda's, and photos, books and other memorabilia of her brothers. For many people, writing to or speaking with Margaret or her mother was akin to being in the company of Patrick or Willie. Margaret was often the recepient of letters from members of the general public who hoped that she could use her political influence to address personal grievances or benefit entitlements; for example, pensions for old IRA members.

Although Margaret and Mary Brigid's relationship was a strained one, Margaret kept in regular contact with other members of her extended family. She wrote to her niece Sr Mary Bridget McGloughlin in Texas, her cousin, Mary Kate Shovelton (née Kelly) and Mary Kate's daughter Désirée Love, both of whom lived in Britain, and her godsons Henry Noel Scarlett (grandson of her half-brother James Vincent) and Colm de Barra, who were frequent visitors to St Enda's.

Aside from letter writing, Margaret's time and energy was consumed by the running of St Enda's. Despite its closure in 1935, Margaret retained links with past pupils and staff members and retained her enthusiasm for educational matters. When James O'Byrne, a former teacher at St Enda's, established Árd Scoil Éanna in Crumlin in 1939, Margaret loaned him school furniture from St Enda's and taught religion there until permanent teachers were recruited. She also had a special interest in initiatives helping children who left leave school early because of familial or financial circumstances.[27]

Throughout the 1940s and 1950s, she consistently struggled to meet the costs of maintaining an eighteenth-century house and its extensive grounds. Her financial woes were compounded by the fact that, over two decades after Patrick's death, she was still repaying his debts. When Patrick was executed in 1916, his debts were c£2,075 and there was only £140 to divide among his creditors. This debt remained with the family after his death and even after the closure of St Enda's in 1935. Margaret often had difficulty paying the rates and, in October 1941, she wrote to de Valera explaining her predicament but reassuring him that the rates would be paid as soon as possible and that St Enda's would be debt free.[28] Financial assistance was not forthcoming from the State and she often relied on friends to pay rates and other debts.

On one occasion, her friend, Fr Senan Moynihan (editor of the *Capuchin Annual*) paid the County Commissioner £150 to cover rate arrears. Margaret was in poor health at this time and wrote to Fr Senan conveying her gratitude to him for settling her outstanding bill.[29] In view of the friendship Margaret and de Valera shared and the fact that St Enda's would become the property of the State on her death, it is surprising that a concession was not made in her case. It is of course possible that de Valera was not cognisant of the true extent of Margaret's debts and that pride forbade her from seeking his assistance. In any case, she remained steadfastly loyal to de Valera during this period and was frequently pictured with him at commemorative events and Fianna Fáil gatherings.

Margaret regarded the four loves in her life as her God, her country, her 'chief' (de Valera) and her alma mater, the Holy Faith School, Clarendon Street. She was appointed honorary life president of the Holy Faith Past Pupils' Union and took a keen interest in educational developments at the congregation's schools in Ireland and abroad. A fellow past pupil of the Holy Faith spoke fondly of Margaret and the high esteem in which she was held. She was regarded as 'the dearest name' on its Roll book and her fellow past pupils 'admired her simplicity, kindness, her steadfast devotion to the Pope and all he represented'.[30]

A devout Catholic, Margaret was a member of many Catholic organisations, including the Catholic Women's Federation and the Pioneer Total Abstinence Association. As early as 1900, she had made her first pilgrimage to Rome, where she received a set of rosary beads from Pope Leo XIII. Margaret also made numerous pilgrimages to Lourdes and in 1932, attended the 31st International Eucharistic Congress in Dublin. In 1947 she wrote a short article entitled 'How to serve mass, with liturgical prayers from the missal', which was published in the *Irish Messenger*. In the article she outlined the steps involved in assisting the priest in serving the mass and encouraged children to incorporate prayer into their daily lives; she believed it was an honour for a child to serve mass.[31]

In April 1950, Margaret travelled to France and Italy with a group of twenty pilgrims, including the Lord Mayor of Dublin, Dr Cormac Breathnach, Fr Senan Moynihan, who acted as spiritual advisor on the trip and Fr Gerald O'Boyle (Margaret's confessor). The group visited Nevers, Lourdes, Paray-le-Monial (where Margaret delighted in visiting the shrine of Saint Margaret Mary Alacoque), Assisi, Padua, Lisieux and Rome. Some days before she was due to depart, however, Margaret broke three ribs. Unfortunately as her ribs had to be strapped, she was unable to wear a corset and, consequently, she could not wear her beloved taffeta dress for the group's private audience with Pope Pius XII on 5 April 1950. Instead, she had to wear a thirty-year-old black dress which upset her greatly. One of her fellow-pilgrims, Thomas MacGreevy, commented on how serene Margaret appeared during the visit and how elegant she looked in her 'gleaming black dress' which he believed was made from a material called 'watered silk'.[32] Margaret had a pragmatic approach to fashion and her style was best described as old-fashioned; her black dress was not 'gleaming' but rather well worn. The pilgrims presented Pope Pius XII with a gold chalice and he in turn presented them with a souvenir medal and rosary beads.

On Easter Monday, 10 April 1950, they breakfasted at the Irish Embassy in Rome. Margaret wondered, '[w]ho on Easter Monday, 1916, could have visualised a group of Irish people being entertained by our Ambassador to the Vatican on Easter Monday, 1950!'[33] Margaret enjoyed her trip to Rome and marvelled at the grandeur of the city, its magnificent ruins, its many churches; she commented that '[n]othing ever written can convey an adequate idea of its beauty and magnificence'.[34] Despite witnessing some of the most beautiful scenery in Europe on her trip, Dublin was never far from Margaret's mind. When she arrived in the Bay of Naples, she was reminded of Dublin Bay and Killiney Bay, noting that '[a]ll the time we were in Naples my mind dwelt on the refrain of the old song: "O Bay of Dublin, my heart you're troublin', Your memory haunts me like a fevered dream".'[35] Her patriotic fervour was also sparked on the trip when an American passenger on a train journey from Italy to Switzerland complimented Margaret and her fellow travellers on their wonderful English sense of humour, she quickly corrected her and pointed out that being mistaken for English was Irish people's 'penalty for speaking a foreign language'.[36]

Margaret remained in contact throughout her life with a number of the priests who had been her brothers' friends, including Fr Joseph Smith, an ardent supporter of the Gaelic League and fluent Irish speaker, and Fr Eugene Nevin, a Passionist priest from Mount Argus who was Patrick and Willie's confessor. Another Passionist priest who was a close friend and confidant of Margaret's was Fr Gerald O'Boyle of St Paul's Retreat, Mount Argus; he was also her Confessor for fifty-four years. Fr O'Boyle was a fervent nationalist who sympathised with the aspirations of the leaders of the 1916 Rising, but did not involve himself in their activities.[37] He excelled in his role as a counsellor and confessor and was regarded by many of his life-long penitents as an *anam cara* (soul friend).[38] When he died on 29 March 1968, Margaret was unable to attend his funeral but sent a message to the Order commending his life-long friendship.

Margaret was an active member of several charitable organisations. She was also a generous benefactor, but, as Éamonn de Barra observed, because of her humble nature, few people knew the extent of her charitable contributions. He stated that '[e]ven when she was hard pressed financially herself I have known her to dispense donations to what she regarded as deserving causes. I greatly fear that on many occasions her unquestioning generosity was imposed upon.'[39] Margaret wrote annual letters to the newspapers appealing for funds for the Ladies' Association of the Charity of St Vincent de Paul, which was attached to St Mary's Pro-Cathedral, Dublin. The Association, founded in 1851 by Margaret Aylward, assisted elderly women living alone and widows with young and sick children. Margaret was an active member of the St Andrew's branch of St Vincent de Paul, which provided clothing, food and fuel to the indigent of Dublin.[40] She joined the association as a teenager because she believed that the work of this charity was crucial to many people who were not entitled to the Old Age, Widows' or Orphans' Pensions at this time.

She was a founder member of the Rathfarnham branch of the Red Cross (established 1940), holding various positions, including president and chairperson. Between 1941 and 1945, she turned St Enda's into a first-aid hospital for Irish soldiers returning from the Second World War. In January 1965, she was awarded a certificate from the Irish Red Cross Association in recognition of her commitment to the organisation; it was presented by Patrick Burke TD, chairman of the Irish Red Cross Association, at a ceremony in Linden Convalescent Home, Blackrock, Co. Dublin. On that occasion, Burke praised Margaret for being 'completely unselfish' and helping 'the nation in every way she could'.[41]

In her spare time, Margaret, like most of her family, loved to read. Her preferred reading material was religious books and historical romances but towards the end of her life she developed a penchant for detective stories. She subscribed for many years to various French magazines to maintain her fluency of the language and read the *Irish Press* daily to keep abreast of current and public affairs, declaring that to handle any of the other newspapers would be a 'National Heresy'.[42] Margaret favoured radio over television, but always enjoyed watching the GAA All-Ireland hurling and football finals. Two months before her death in 1968, she cheered from her home at St Enda's as the Wexford hurlers defeated Tipperary 5-8 to 3-12 in the final at Croke Park in Dublin.[43] One of Margaret's favourite radio programmes was Paddy Crosbie's 'School around the corner' and she often spoke of her desire to appear on the show.[44] Margaret was proud of her Dublin roots and appreciated the unique Dublin sense of humour.

She enjoyed Dubliner Jimmy O'Dea's comedy sketches on the radio and television, and attended many of his shows at the Gaiety and Olympia theatres.

Although Margaret never married, she had an active social life and wide circle of friends. In company, she delighted in recounting anecdotes about her brothers and she had many willing listeners who were content to listen to intimate details of the childhood of Patrick and Willie. At the monthly meetings of the Past Pupils' Union, after methodically going through each item on the agenda, Margaret was often prompted to relate stories of the young Pearses.

Margaret was admitted to the Linden Convalescent Home, Blackrock, several times during the last decade of her life. As her health deteriorated, it became necessary to reduce her public appearances. In October 1961, she wrote to Fianna Fáil Lord Mayor Robert Briscoe to say that she was unable to speak at an election rally due to illness. Knowing that the letter would be published in the *Irish Press*, she used the opportunity to appeal to voters to return Fianna Fáil with a clear majority.[45] In 1962, she was unable to attend the Annual Pearse Commemoration Concert at the Royal Hibernian Hotel, Dublin, but sent a tape-recorded message encouraging those in attendance to speak Irish.[46]

Margaret sold Cullenswood House to the State in 1960 alleviating some financial worries. The proceeds of the sale were used to repay the mortgage, to settle outstanding debts, and, in accordance with Mrs Pearse's will, to pay for the celebraton of masses for the deceased members of her family. Margaret still struggled to maintain St Enda's on her salary from the Seanad and was increasingly reliant on her friends for financial support. She shared her concerns for the future of St Enda's with her neighbour, barrister and Irish language activist, Pádraig Ó Siocháin. Ó Siocháin tried to establish a fundraising committee for St Enda's but was unsuccessful; he later funded the installation of a heating system in the house. In the final decade of her life, Margaret became increasingly unhappy with the lack of support from her

Fianna Fáil colleagues. She believed the government had neglected St Enda's for many years and doubted that they would care for it properly after her death.[47] In March 1966, there was speculation in the press that instead of bequeathing St Enda's to the State, in accordance with her mother's will, she was considering leaving it to a religious order, the Archbishop of Dublin, or the Cheshire Homes.[48]

Though Margaret did not make a formal statement, the issue was raised in Dáil Éireann by Michael O'Leary, a Labour TD. O'Leary was concerned that, despite the payment by the Office of Public Works of approximately £7,800 on repairs to the roof, boundary walls and other works, the government had no guarantee that St Enda's would become the property of the State following Margaret's death.[49] Despite negotiations between the Department of Finance and Margaret (from her sick bed), the matter was not resolved before the fiftieth anniversary commemoration of the 1916 Rising.

Margaret was unable to attend the official commemoration of the Rising on 10 April 1966, of which her grand-nephew, Piaras MacLochlainn (son of Alfred McGloughlin and keeper of the museum at Kilmainham Gaol), was the organising secretary. She watched the celebrations on television at the Linden Convalescent Home and students from Kilternan National School staged a pageant of the Rising for her at the Home, which included readings of works by Patrick. The following day, Margaret was brought to St Patrick's Hall, Dublin Castle, to receive her honorary Doctorate of Law, which was conferred on her by Éamon de Valera, Chancellor of the National University. She was in poor health and rested on a stretcher for the duration of the ceremony. Five other relatives of signatories of the Proclamation were also honoured on that occasion, namely, Rónán E. Ceannt (son of Éamonn Ceannt), Donagh MacDonagh (son of Thomas MacDonagh), Geraldine Dillon (sister of Joseph Plunkett), Senator Nora Connolly O'Brien (daughter of James Connolly) and Kathleen Clarke.[50] After the ceremony, Margaret asked Éamonn de Barra to drive her around the city; de Barra later remarked that 'she enjoyed the city tour in 1966 more than the elaborate conferring ceremonial in Dublin Castle'.[51]

Meanwhile Margaret's health was deteriorating further and she was anxious about St Enda's and how much longer she could fulfil her obligations to her mother's will. In consultation with Pádraig Ó Siocháin, Luke McKeogh (auctioneer and past pupil of St Enda's) and Margaret's solicitor John Maher, it was decided to put pressure on the government to alleviate her financial pressures. On 19 September 1966, an advertisement for the sale of eleven acres at St Enda's appeared in the *Irish Press*.[52] The threatened sale caused some consternation in government circles and Charles Haughey, then Minister for Finance, arranged urgent discussions with Margaret regarding the future of the house. After lengthy negotiations, the government agreed to pay Margaret a sum of £22,000 for eleven acres of St Enda's on condition that she signed the house, land and other properties on the estate over to the State. Margaret duly signed an indenture gifting St Enda's (the house, lands and contents) to the State after her death and an official statement to that effect was made on 1 February 1967.

From early 1967 onwards, Margaret spent lengthy periods at the Linden Convalescent Home. Despite this, she participated in a debate calling for an end to live hare coursing. In a letter to the *Irish Press*, Margaret expressed her revulsion at the practice 'in which greyhounds literally tear the poor little defenceless hare asunder'.[53] She asserted that her brothers, Patrick and Willie, would not have condoned such inhumane treatment of animals. In March of that year there were reports in the press that she was 'very weak' and her friends feared that she would not last long; she rallied, however, and her recovery was celebrated in the *Irish Press* under the heading 'Miss Pearse improves'.[54] Margaret was regularly visited by TDs and dignitaries during her time at the Linden Convalescent Home. De Valera, who celebrated with her on her eighty-ninth and ninetieth birthdays, later declared 'Is minic a bhíodh tuarscáil na Dála roimpi ar a leaba nuair a chuaigh mise amach chun í a fheiceáil'[55] ('Often when I came to visit her, she was surrounded by members of the Dáil'). These TDs kept her abreast of political life and, when a reporter from the *Irish Independent* interviewed her on her eighty-ninth birthday, she informed him that she 'was satisfied that the country was making very good progress towards the State which the 1916 men had visualised'.[56] On Margaret's ninetieth birthday, Taoiseach Jack Lynch sent her greetings from Bombay; Charles Haughey called to the nursing home; and birthday messages were sent by the Lord Mayors of Dublin, Cork, and Wexford, and from individuals and organisations nationally and internationally.

In May 1968, Margaret was brought by ambulance from the Linden Convalescent Home to Áras an Uachtaráin to have afternoon tea with de Valera, his wife Sinéad, and their guests, the King and Queen of Belgium. This was in recognition of Margaret's visit to Belgium with her brother in 1905 to investigate bilingual methods of education. Margaret returned to St Enda's for one last trip shortly before her death and was accompanied by Maureen Breen, her secretary and companion of twenty-four years, and her Alsatian dog. She was readmitted to Linden a month before her death and died there, aged ninety, on 7 November 1968 in the presence of Sisters Agnes and Columba of the Sisters of Charity, who had nursed her through previous illnesses.

From documents housed at the National Archives of Ireland, it is evident that preparations for a State funeral for Margaret were set in motion as early as 1960. The plan entitled 'Senator Margaret M. Pearse: Official action in event of death' was proposed by senior civil servants at the Department of Defence to the Tánaiste Seán MacEntee and later sanctioned by An Taoiseach Seán Lemass in October 1960. The proposal was that, in the event of Margaret's death, there should be full military participation in the funeral including a funeral escort comprising of two companies with colour party, the army band, a bearer party of six military policemen, church pall bearers and a guard of honour, and a strong military presence at Glasnevin Cemetery. In keeping with

protocol on the death of a member of the Seanad, the flag over
Leinster House would be flown at half mast and the Cathaoirleach
would make an official statement of condolence on the day of her
death. It was stated that President de Valera would make a graveside
oration. What is of most interest in this correspondence is how
eager Fianna Fáil officials were to hijack Margaret's funeral and
turn it into a dramatic public event which would forever associate
the sacrifice of the Pearse family and the legacy of 1916 with
their party. This was all, of course, dependent on whether or not
Fianna Fáil would be in government at the time of her death, and
fortunately for them, they were.

The news of Margaret's death featured prominently in
contemporary newspapers and the clichéd language employed
was reminiscent of that used in obituaries for her mother over
three decades previously. The *Irish Times* described her as a 'servant
of the nation',[57] and the *Irish Independent* marked her passing by
stating that '[t]he last survivor of an honourable and gallant Irish
family has been laid to rest with the fullest homage and ceremony
with which the Nation could pay its final tribute'.[58] Leading
politicians mourned her loss and lamented that the strongest link
with Easter Week was broken. De Valera's comment that she 'was
a woman of great intellectual capacity and a woman of an iron
will' seemed impersonal in light of the fact that he had been a
close family friend for over fifty years.[59] Perhaps her actions in the
last decade of her life were an embarrassment to him; in any case,
he chose not to deliver the graveside oration.

As planned, Margaret's funeral was a spectacular public event.
As her remains were removed to the Church of the Annunciation,
Rathfarnham, a guard of honour was mounted along Linden's
avenue by students of Carysfort Training College and the Dublin
Brigade of the Old IRA. En route to the church, the funeral
cortège briefly paused as it passed the gates of St Enda's. The State
funeral on 9 November was celebrated in Irish by her friend Fr
Tom Walsh OP, Chaplain to the Dublin Brigade of the Old IRA.
The chief mourners included Désirée Love, Patrick Shovelton,

members of the McGloughlin and Scarlett families, Tom, William and Michael Pearse and Maureen Breen. Éamon de Valera, Jack Lynch, Cormac Breslin (Ceann Comhairle), Liam Cosgrave (Fine Gael leader), Chief Justice Cearbhall Ó Dálaigh, Lord Mayor Alderman Frank Cluskey and army Chief of Staff, Lt General Seán McEoin attended the requiem mass. Also in attendance were government ministers, members of the Dáil, Seanad, Council of State, Dublin Corporation, the Old IRA, former staff and past pupils of St Enda's and Holy Faith schools; former members of Na Fianna and Cumann na mBan and her colleagues at the Red Cross, Catholic Women's Federation and Conradh na Gaeilge.

The choir of Holy Cross College, Clonliffe, sang and as her coffin draped in the Tricolour was carried from the church, the No. 1 Army Band played Thomas Moore's 'Remember the Glories of Brien the Brave'. Two hundred boys and girls from St Enda's High School and Árd Scoil Éanna provided a guard of honour as the hearse left the church. The cortège stopped for a minute's silence on the way to Glasnevin at the GPO, where hundreds gathered to pay their respects. As they approached the gates of the cemetery, the Army Band played the 'Celtic Lament'. Jack Lynch delivered a very brief graveside oration.

> Miss Pearse's life, like that of her patriot brothers, Pádraic and Willie, was dedicated to Ireland. She had an abiding and passionate love of country and was a most sincere and devoted advocate of every cause that was noble and good. Her patriotic zeal, her love of Ireland, her great Christian charity, her love for the poor, her deep concern for those in need – these are some of the great characteristics which endeared Miss Pearse to all who were privileged to know her and for which she will always be affectionately remembered.

> Whether as a member of the Dáil or Seanad or of the Fianna Fáil National Executive, Miss Pearse brought to

bear on all her activities the same sense of dedication, the same sense of noble purpose and the same conscientious discharge of duty which always guided her and which so inspired all who knew and revered her.

As Uachtarán na hÉireann, who for so long shared her labours and her suffering, has said in his own tribute to her, the strongest link with the heroic men of Easter Week has now been broken. Ireland is the poorer for her death.

Pádraic Pearse's own moving words at Rossa's grave seem singularly appropriate as we gather round the grave of his beloved sister. We, too, like the mourners of O'Donovan Rossa, stand at this grave "not in sadness but rather in exaltation of spirit that it has been given to us to come thus into so close a communion with that brave and splendid Gael".

This grave also, and historic St Enda's, which Miss Pearse had arranged should on her death become the property of the Nation, will, I am sure, be always places of pilgrimage and sources of inspiration for future generations of Irish men and women who will revere the memory of Margaret Pearse and carve her name with pride.[60]

Margaret was buried in the Pearse family plot, along with her mother, father and sister.

She left an estate worth £6,036. She bequeathed £1,000 and some personal belongings to Maureen Breen and cash sums to Florence Scarlett, Thomas Pearse, Elizabeth Raftery (Linden Convalescent Home), Éamonn de Barra, Lillian Nally and Mary Kennedy. Much of her estate was left to charitable causes such as the Irish Sisters of Charity, the Sisters of Mercy Night Shelter for Women, the Night Shelter for Men, the Sick and Indigent Roomkeepers Society, the French Sisters of Charity for Our

Lady's Home, and the Sisters of the Holy Faith.[61] She bequeathed St Enda's to the nation, as a memorial to her brothers, with two conditions attached, namely, that it would remain open all year round and that no admission fee would be charged.

At a ceremony on 23 April 1970, de Valera accepted the keys of St Enda's from Éamonn de Barra (chairman of Cumann na bPiarsach) and John Maher (Pearse family solicitor) on behalf of the State. Members of Pearse's 'E' Company and the Old IRA attended along with past pupils and former staff of St Enda's.[62] The Pearse Museum, under the care of the Office of Public Works was opened to the public by President Patrick Hillery on 10 November 1979 – the centenary of Patrick Pearse's birth.

CONCLUSION

People will say hard things of us now, but later on will praise us ... dear Mother. May God bless you for your great love for me and for your great faith in me, and may He remember all that you have so bravely suffered. I hope soon to see Papa, and in a little while we shall be all together again. 'Wow-wow,' Willie, Mary Brigid, and Mother, good-bye. I have not words to tell you of my love for you and home, and how my heart yearns to you all.[1]

Patrick Pearse

In truth, few people were genuinely concerned with the griefs or woes of Margaret, Mary Brigid or their mother in the years following the executions of Patrick and Willie. If the 1916 Rising was a defining moment in the lives of Patrick and Willie, it was life changing for the Pearse women. After the Rising, they were dehumanised, lived constantly in the shadow of Patrick and Willie, and were increasingly only valued for their symbolic importance as the surviving family of Patrick Pearse. They were given no chance to grieve or deal with their traumatic losses but were expected to play their parts in the creation and maintenance of public myths surrounding the 1916 Rising. They became acceptable and respectable representatives of a brutal and divisive rebellion and important tools in the creation of a republican lineage for the Fianna Fáil party. Margaret and her mother were uncontroversial figures who towed the party line and their appearance at a rally, meeting or State occasion was the ultimate endorsement of any cause.

Mary Brigid questioned and was often frustrated by the legacy of the Rising. She spent much of her life trying to reconcile why her beloved Patrick would abandon a loving family for his political ideals. On the contrary, Margaret unquestiongly, often blindly, supported her brothers' decisions and accepted the consequences of their actions. She was a formidable, well-educated, intelligent woman who could have achieved success in any career she chose. She had a long career in politics, but her poltical career was built solely on the Pearse connection. At heart, she was an educationalist and one can't help but wonder how different her path in life might have been had she remained at her preparatory school for girls and boys in Donnybrook and developed some of the teaching methods and techniques which she applied there. Instead, she relinquished her personal ambitions and aspirations and embraced Patrick's philosophy that viewed sacrifice as an integral part of nationalism.

As Patrick and Willie were absorbed into the hagiography of Irish patriots after the Rising, their family was initially viewed by many in quasi-religious terms as the living embodiment of patriotic sacrifice. Some commentators have blamed Margaret and her mother for claiming ownership of the Rising, which caused resentment amongst other bereaved families, and of perpetuating some of the distorted myths, particularly surrounding Patrick and the Rising. Margaret and her mother lived in a vacuum and their loyalty to Patrick and Willie and what they perceived as their patriotic duty to the State may have forbade them from questioning those around them who constantly fed them lines about 'sacrifice', patriotism and the cause of Irish freedom. Over fifty years after the Rising, Margaret received a letter written by a nun from the Convent of the Sacred Heart, Roscrea, thanking her for the 'glorious but terrible sacrifice' made by her and her family in 1916 and admitting that she was still in awe of them.[2]

Margaret's death in 1968 at the age of ninety years marked the end of the Pearse family's active involvement in Irish politics, education and culture. In her final years, she felt increasingly isolated at St Enda's and feared that 'old retainers and relatives' were waiting for her demise so they could rummage through and remove the contents of the house. She believed employees and a tenant on the estate were stealing from her and described families who were living rent free in lodges on the estate as being 'hostile'.[3] After a long life, one wonders what thoughts were in her mind in the days and weeks before her death. Was she consoled by memories of the loving security of the old house in Great Brunswick Street? Did she wonder how ordinary children with a fondness for staging plays, playing pranks, and baking cakes, could have followed such unusual paths in life? Did she regret devoting her entire life to the perpetuation of her brother's ideals and their legacy, or did she just accept it as the burden of being a Pearse?

'The Old Grey Mare'

At break of day, I chanced to stray
All by the Seine's fair side,
When to ease my heart young Bonaparte
Came forward now to ride.
On a field of green with gallant mien
He formed his men in square,
And down the line with look so fine
He rode his Old Grey Mare.

My sporting boys that's tall and straight,
Take counsel and be wise,
Attention pay to what I say,
My lecture don't despise:
Let patience guide you everywhere,
And from traitors now beware,
For there's none but men that's sound within
Can ride my Old Grey Mare.

Bonaparte on her did start,
He rode too fast, it's true!
She lost a shoe at Moscow fair

And got lame at Waterloo.
But wait till she comes back to the shamrock shore
Where she'll get farriers' care,
And at the very next gate she'll win the plate,
My sporting Old Grey Mare!

Catalogue of Literary Works by Mary Brigid Pearse

The Murphys of Ballystack	Dublin: M.H. Gill, 1917
'The life of Pádraig Pearse'	*Our Boys* magazine, 15 April 1926–20 January 1927
The Home-Life of Pádraig Pearse	Dublin: Browne and Nolan, 1934
When You Come Home	Novel, short story and radio play
Curly and the Persian	Novel and short story
The Romance of Castle Bawn	Novel and series in *Irish Catholic*, April and October 1931
Luck	Play
Over the Stile	Play
Diplomacy	Play
The Shamrock Girl	Play
The King's Jester	Play

The Manuscript	Play
The Saint of Aran	Play
The Message	Play
The King's Ransome	Play
Geese	Play
Triumph	Play
Brian Boru	Play
The Good People	Play
The Tinnscra	Play
St Enda's	Play

Charles Dickens adaptations:

The Chimes	Play
The Cricket on the Hearth	Play
Barnaby Rudge	Play
The Baron of Grogzwig	Play
'Untitled'	Play set outside Lughna's Dun, Co. Galway
'Untitled'	Play (first line: Enter Baron very dejected)
The Path of Light	Play/short story
The Open Door	Radio play
The Meetin'	Radio play
Two Shots in the Dark	Radio play and short story

Curtain Up	Short story
Ingle Nooks	Short story
Lumen de Lumene	Short story
A Fantastic Fantasy	Short story
Gossips	Short story
The Fairies Glen	Short story
The Pipe of Peace	Short story
A Spring Song	Short story
A Bank Holiday	Short story
The Lie	Short story
Wanted – a Grandmother	Short story
St Brigid's/The Shield	Short story
Some Un-seasonable Remarks	Short story
Old Timsey's St Patrick's Pot	Short story
Theeseya	Short story
The Understudy	Short story
First Class	Short story
St Brigid's Procession	Short Story
The Life Story of a Saintly Irish Maiden – Kathleen Kirwan	Short story
An Sagart	Short story in *The Cross* 7, no. 7 (October 1916)

All of St Patrick's Day	Short story in *Our Girls: the magazine for the girls of Ireland*, 1, no. 6, March 1931)
Happy Days	Unfinished
Foolish Fun	Unfinished
Some impressions of the Eucharistic Congress Week by a Dubliner	Essay
A Visit to Rosmuc with Patrick Pearse	Essay

APPENDIX 3

Scene 1, *Over the Stile* by Mary Brigid Pearse

OVER THE STILE

A Comedy in one act.

Time, present

Characters.

Pat Casey... A strong farmer.

Nan Casey.. His wife.

Katie Casey...His daughter.

Peggy Casey ....His daughter.

Barney O'Hara .... His head man.

Alec McKenna...A Scotch field hand.

Mat ....A wandering fiddler.

Scene I

Outside Pat's cottage. Time, evening in Autumn.

Back cloth, corn fields in Autumn tints; brown and red. Right; cottage.

A bench in front of door. Left, back, a stile, leading into the fields.

Pat discovered sitting on bench, smoking. Katie near him, with a spinning wheel. A bird sings. Alec comes slowly on stage, on the FAR side of stile, and, leaning on the stile, listens to the bird.

PAT. (Taking the pipe from his mouth) Is that Alec McKenna beyant at the stile, Katie?

KATIE. It is, father.

PAT. An' wat may he be doin' there, I wondher, whin it's cuttin' the corn he should be?

KATIE. Cuttin' the corn, an' it goin' to nine o'clock! Shure, a boy can't be for ever workin'!

PAT. Alec McKenna doesn't be for iver workin' even if he can, itself! 'Tis listenin' to the birds singin' ('The wee birdies,' He calls thim) an' watchin' the butherflies he does be! 'Twould answer him betther to help your mother to make the butther-MILK, an' lave the butther-FLIES alone!

KATIE. He's a great hand at the learnin', right enough, but – but – he takes his full share of the work with all. Barney O'Hara says so, an an' – it's Barney is the smart boy!

PAT. (In disgust) Musha! But 'tis the purty face an' the blarneyin' tongue that gets round a woman!

KATIE. An' what gets round a man?

PAT. It all depinds on the SOORT av a man it is, allanna; bud there's only the WAN soort av woman, an' she's the same the wide world over! (Smokes)

KATIE. (Aside, and sighing) I wish I knew the way to get round YOUR sort of a man then, for it's mighty hard thryin'!

PAT. Katie! Do ye know that Alec – that Alec – wants to meet ye daown be the ould bridge to-morra evenin' at five o'clock? Or – er THERE – abouts! (He stops smoking)

KATIE. Won't he be in the corn fields, father?

PAT. (Stammeringly) He – he – axed me to let him off – early – an' – an' (Begins to cough)

KATIE. (Anxiously) What's the matter, father? Have ye a cold?

PAT. No then, I – I haven't! It's – it's the smokin', Katie. It vint against me breath, so it did.

KATIE. But you're not smokin', father.

PAT. No, – I'm not – So I see that bud I – thought I was. It's something that tickles me throat, Katie! That's what it is! Bud it's nothin' to be onaisy about.

KATIE. I thought you didn't like Peggy or me talkin' to the men.

PAT. Neither I don't; bud he axed me so-er-Hard, like, that I hadn't the heart to say him no.

KATIE. Now, I wonder what he'll be saying' to me!

PAT. Mabbe he'll be tellin' ye something about buttherflys an' the like.

KATIE. But what good will that be to one or the other of us?

PAT. Not a ha'porth av good! Bud it's the soort av thing a quare, poor fool like Alec would be sayin' to a girl.

KATIE. But, father –

NAN. (Inside the cottage, calling) Katie! Katie!

PAT. (Quickly) Run into your mother, like a good girl, an' get the supper bud don't forget about to-morra.

KATIE. I won't father, but –

NAN. (Inside) Katie! Where are ye, me darlin'?

KATIE. I'm comin' mother.

(Goes into the cottage. Pat chuckles heartily, and Alec comes slowly down stage)

ALEC. (Raising his cap) Good-evening, Mr Casey.

PAT. Good-evenin' to ye, Alec. Fine weather we're havin'.

ALEC. Grand, sir.

PAT. I've a message to ye, from me daughter, Alec! She wants ye to meet her to-morra evenin' at a quarter to six, be the ould Well, below the river. She – she –

(He begins to cough. Alec pats him on the back)

ALEC. You've a bad cough, Mr Casey.

PAT. I can't say I have, thin! 'Tis something catches me in the wind pipe, sudden like. It's – it's the heavy dews, I'll go bail.

ALEC. They're very heavy these nights, Mr Casey.

PAT. (Aside) O! The gomeral! He doesn't see I'm makin' a fool av him!

(To Alec) Ye'll be meetin' me daughter, won't ye? I'll let ye off from the fields early, wid a heart an' a half!

ALEC. Thank ye, Mr Casey. But I wonder what she wants to say to me!

PAT. Mebbe 'tis something abouts Black Beetles, Alec! She has a morthal dread av thim, howsomeever.

ALEC. (Surprised) But what good would it be to tell ME about them?

PAT. No good at all; bud 'tis the contrary ways women do be havin'! Wanst they get a notion the divil himself couldn't get out av thim. The QUARER the notion, the Harder it does be to destroy it: an' it might be yourself that ud be destroyed if ye THRIED to get it out!

(Katie puts her head out over the half door of the cottage)

KATIE. Supper is ready, father.

PAT. (Gets up) Well, good–night, Alec.

ALEC. (Raising his cap again) Good-night, sir. (Goes off, right. Pat sits down again, chuckling.)

NAN. (Looking over the half door) Will ye come in to your supper, like a good man? The stir-a-bout is sittin' on the hob, waitin' on ye.

PAT. Wait a minit, Nan! I want to spake to ye.

NAN. The stir-a-bout 'ill be spoilt on me.

PAT. Woman dear, 'twill ne only coolin' itself! Sit down here, till I talk soft to ye.

(Nan comes out of cottage, and sits beside him knitting)

PAT. Don't yr think, Nan, that it's high time Katie an' Peggy wor settled?

NAN. (Doubtfully) I – I don't know, thin: they're young yet, an' we'll miss thim sore whin they're gone.

PAT. We will, shure enough! Bud WE aren't so young as we used to be, we must think av THIM, Nan.

NAN. (Sorrowfully) Ay, that's thrue! Is there anywan in particular that you're thinkin' about, Pat?

PAT. There's Brian Doolin, an' Nat Finnigan, who'd make great matches for the girls: Bud before it's settled, I'm to give thim all a coolin'!

NAN. (Anxiously) But, Pat; I – I'm thinkin' that Peggy cares for young Barney O'Hara!

PAT. (Indignantly) An' do ye think, woman, wan av Pat Casey's daughters can't do bether nor marry wan av her father's field hands?

NAN. (Indignantly) She might do WORSE! Barney's a good lad, wid a fine face an' figure av his own!

PAT. (Scornfully) A FINE FACE AN' FIGURE! HOW ARE YE!

Do women niver think av anything bud good looks whin they're afther a husband!

NAN. (Innocently) They do, avourneen; Didn't I take yourself?

PAT. (Shouting) What do ye mane by that, Mrs Casey, ma'am?

NAN. (Alarmed) O! God betune us an' all harm! What are ye shoutin' for, I was only tellin' ye that I married ye, an' there's no sense in getting' vexed over it at this time av the day!

PAT. (Shouting louder) I'm not vexed, woman!!!

NAN. (Standing up, and speaking nervously) Well, if you're not vexed, I'm either dhrunk or dhramin', for ye look leppin' mad this minit!

PAT. (More mad) 'Tis your foolish tongue ud make a cow leppin' mad, Mrs Casey!

NAN. (Dazed) God save us! But he must be sorry he married me at all!

(Puts her apron to her eyes)

PAT. (Pulling her down beside him again) Don't be doin' 'LA' Nan! Now listen to me, avourneen. Doolan 'ill make a fine son-in-law –

NAN. I'd rather have Barney meself!

PAT. It's not what YOU want, Mrs Casey! It's what I want!

NAN. It should be what PEGGY an' KATIE want!

PAT. If ya always give a woman her own way, there'll be the divil to pay!

NAN. An' if ye don't give PEGGY her own way, there'll be the divil to pay in earnest! She's a high spirit, I can tell ye!

PAT. (Testily) Musha, woman, can't ye stop argufyin', an' let me have me say out? I've toult Alec McKenna that he's to meet Katie at the ould Well, to-morra evenin', at a quarter to six;

an' I toult Katie that she's to meet Alec at the Bridge beyant, at five, or so.

NAN. But I thought ye wouldn't let the girls even talk to the boys, much less meet thim! Ye were always afeart they'd get fond av wan another an' get married!

PAT. Have ye no sense at all, woman? There's a great difference betune talkin' an' marryin', I can tell ye!

NAN. (Sighing) There doesn't seem too much difference to-night, anyway!

PAT. Well, then Nan, can't ye be quiet, an' let ME talk!

NAN. But Pat, ma chree, if ye sind the craturs to different places, they 'ill niver meet at all, at all!

PAT. (Chuckling) They will not; an' that's how they'll get a coolin'.

NAN. (Thoughtfully) It's warm weather, Pat; they won't be cool –

PAT. Arrah, Nan, can't see a joke! It's a PRACTICAL joke, don't ye see?

NAN. (Shortly) O! IS it? (Rises) Take care it isn't yourself that'll get the coolin', my good man! (Goes into cottage.)

(Pat goes after her, still chuckling. Peggy heard singing in the distance. She sings first verse of song, gradually coming closer, and crosses the stile, on the stage. She carries a milk pail, and stool)

PEG. (Putting down pail, and throwing stool across the stage) Musha! But's it's a quare world, an' thim that's in it is quarer! It's meself that doesn't know what to make of some of the boys at all! (Starts to mimic Alec) It's 'Good-mornin', Miss Peggy, I – I hope – I mean – the weather is great, intirely'! 'Twas spillin' rain wan day he said that the AMADAWN! MISS PEGGY! Instead of, 'Is that yourself, Peg, avourneen shure, I love ye, an' I want ye to marry ye!' Och! Tatthershion to him. (Pulls off her sun bonnet, in anger, and throws it on the ground) For a dunderhead an' a GANDHER! Shure, a cow would have more sense!

KATIE. (Looking over door) IS that you, Peggy? The supper is stone cold, an' me father is red hot.

PEG. (Flinging herself down on the grass) I don't want any supper.

(Katie disappears, and Peggy croons softly:

I know my love by his way of walking;
I know my love by his way of talking;
And if my love leaves me, what should I do)

PAT. (Coming out of cottage) Step that Gom-actin', Peggy Casey, an' go into your supper at wanst!

PEG. (Slowly rising, and sighing) I wonder when will you learn sinse! (Turns at door, and calls back, tauntingly) But I suppose, it's too much to expect of a misfortunate man!

(Goes into cottage. Pat sits down, and fills his pipe. Stage grows a little darker, and lights appear in the cottage window. Barney, Alec and Mat, come on, and Barney and Alec cross the stile, and come down centre of stage. Mat sits on the stile, and tunes his fiddle softly)

BAR. (Breezily) God save ye, Mr Casey! (Nan comes out of cottage) An' you too, ma'am! (Raises his cap)

NAN. God save ye kindly, a vic.

BAR. Isn't it the grand weather we're havin'?

NAN. It is, thanks be to God.

BAR. AN' how is the world usin' yourself, Mr Casey?

PAT. (Sourly) Och! I have me throubles! An' the biggest is that handful, me daughter Peggy! She's heart scald, an' no mistake, wid her copy cuttin', an' impident tongue!

NAN. O! Pat, a shtor, don't talk that way! Ye know Peggy is a good girl; as good as ye'll find in a month av Sundays! An' BETTHER!

BAR. We came round, Mrs Casey, thinkin' we might have a bit av a dance. Mat –

PAT. Tell him to take himself an' his oul fiddle out av that at wanst. Wouldn't I look the purty fool leppin' an' jiggin' to the scrapin' av a broken fiddle?

BAR. (Cheerfully) Ye would, Mr Casey, fair enough! But –

PAT. (In a rage) Katie! Get me me Black Thorn, till I lay this spalpeen stiff! Ye – ye – brazen young divil, ye! I'LL tach ye to respect your betthers!

(He rushes at Barney, who catches him very gently, and holds him.)

BAR. Easy, now, Mr Casey! I meant no harm in the world!

NAN. (Laying her hand on Pat's arm) Och, Pat, avourneen, don't be mindin' everything! Ye'll desthroy yourself intirely! Come an' sit down, an' have a smoke. (Calls) Peggy! Will ye bring me a sod av live turf to light your father's pipe, like a good girl! (Pat sits down grumbling. Katie comes out with the stick, and Peggy with the turf)

KATIE. What's this for, father?

PAT. It's to hit that bestheen a larrup over the skull with!

KATIE. (Dropping the stick, which strikes Pat's feet) O! God save us!

PAT. (In another rage) Bedam, me fut is broke on me! God give ye sense, girl, for 'tis the foolish wan ye are! I'm a miserable man this day wid me two daughters doin' all they can to make a cripple av me, an' a dominted amadawn! Makin' a tagit av me, so they are for their tongues an' sticks! Me, the father that reared thim, wid niver a cross word comin' out av me lips!

NAN. (Piously) Glory be to God! Am I hearin' right at all!

(Peggy gives her father the turf, and Katie goes shyly over to Barney)

PAT. Where the divil is me pipe, Nan? Some wan has med off wid it!

NAN. Thry the seat your sittin' on, Pat darlint.

PAT. Do ye take your husband for a GOMERAL, woman, that you think I might be sittin' on me own pipe? (Shouts)

NAN. (Sighing) Musha! But 'tis the quare timper ye have, anyway!

PAT. (Mad) I'll not be stoppin' here to be med a fool av be me own wife an' daughters. Be the gonnies, I won't!

(Gets up, and slams into the cottage. Pipe discovered on the seat)

NAN. Shure, 'tis a quare, ould man he is, an' no mistake. I'll give him his dudeen, an' mebbe 'twill put him in a betther timper.

BAR. (Grinning) He couldn't be in a worse wan, anyhow, Ma'am.

(Nan trots into cottage with pipe)

ALEC. (Shyly) Is that yourself, Miss Peggy?

PEG. (Tossing her head) No! It's me sisther!

ALEC. Can't ye say something kind to a boy, Miss Peggy?

PEG. I could – if 'twas the RIGHT boy!

ALEC. (Moving towards her, and almost upsetting the pail of milk) Miss Peggy, I –

PEG. Mind the milk! You'll spill it on me!

(He moves back hastily, and upsets the pail)

ALEC. I – I – I'm very sorry, Miss Peggy –

PEG. (Cuttingly) Och! Don't mention it! It's only what I'd expect from the like av ye!

KATIE. (Gently) O! Peg!!! Don't mind, Mr McKenna. There's plenty more.

BAR. 'Tis yourself is the kind, little colleen, astoir (Tenderly to Katie)

PEG. Let's have a dance, Mr O'Hara. I'm tired of Mr Kenn's grand conversation.

BAR. We'll start at wanst, an' your father can't stop us! Strike up, Mat! (Mat starts tuning loudly)

ALEC. Will ye dance with me, Miss Peggy?

PEG. I'd sooner dance with a broom-stick!

ALEC. (Going to Katie) Miss Katie, will YOU dance with me?

BAR. (Catching her, and whirling her away) No, she won't, me boy! She's goin' to dance with me.

PEG. Well, sooner than not dance at all, I'll dance with you, Mr McKenna.

(They form up for a reel)

PAT. (Putting his head over the door) I tell ye, I'll have no jiggin'!

PEG. It's a reel, father!

PAT. (Shouting) Peggy Casey! I'll –

NAN. Aisy, Pat, or ye'll hurt yourself.

(They go back into cottage, and the reflection on the window grows brighter as if a fire were been blown up inside. Mat begins to play, 'The Wind that Shakes the Barley', and they dance. Nan comes out, and sits down to knit)

PAT. (Putting his head out through the little, open window) Nan! Didn't I tell ye I'd have no dancin'?

NAN. What harm is there in a dance, Pat?

PAT. Am I masther in me own house, or am I not? Answer me that, Mrs Casey.

NAN. Musha, have sense, man alive an' don't be botherin' yourself. Come out here, an' the air 'ill do ye god, avourneen.

(Pat comes out, and sits beside her, smoking)

PAT. (Pointing scornfully at Alec) Shire, that GOM can't dance! Look at the long legs av him, an' the wooden face, for all the world like a dilapidated pot stick!

NAN. Whist! He'll hear ye! (She keeps time to the dance, with her feet, and hums softly)

PAT. Sorra the bit I care if he does!

NAN. But HE'LL care! An' I think it's a purty sight to see thim all dancin'.

PAT. It is not, Mrs Casey, Ma'am! 'Tis a foolish sight to see thim all leppin' about like hins on a hot griddle!

NAN. (Still keeping time, and even waving her knitting in time to her own dancing feet) Well, DON'T look at thim, then! (Barney gives the usual whoop, as he dances, and Peg does the same)

PAT. (Scornfully) Listen to the shouts av thim!

NAN. O, Pat! Can't ye be aisy!

PAT. Can't THEY be aisy! Och! There's me ould pipe out on me now. (He goes in to relight his pipe. Nan gets up, and does a little dance all by herself, very quietly, before the seat. Pat, coming back, regards her in blank astonishment)

PAT. Is it takin' lave av your senses ye are, woman? Leppin' about like as if ye had the jigs!

NAN. (Breathless sinking on the seat) O! God love me. It makes me feel young again!

PAT. (Unpleasantly) It makes ye LOOK oulder, thin!

(He sits and smokes in sullen silence, until the dance is finished. Then he stands up, and shakes his stick threateningly at the fiddler)

PAT. If I catch ye here again, Mat, I'll make ye play another tune! An' so I'm tellin' ye!

BAR. (Calmly) Thank ye, Mat! Now we'll be goin', Mrs Casey. Good-night to ye, ma'am. Good-night, Mr Casey! Good-night all.

NAN. Good-night, a vic. Safe home, Alec!

(Pat goes into cottage, and Nan follows. Barney kisses Katie, who goes in quickly. Alec trys to shake hands with Peggy, but she ignores him. They cross the stile, and Mat and Barney go off. Alec pauses, and looks back. But she makes no sign, and he goes off, too.)

PEG. (Humming softly) O! Wouldn't I like to be over the stile,

Over the stile! Over the stile!

O! Wouldn't I like to see somebody smile,

And coming coming – to meet me!

(She breaks down suddenly; and going over the stile, she sits on the lowest step, resting her head on the other step. She weeps bitterly. Stage darkens, and the harvest crescent moon appears in the sky)

Tableau

N.B. The melody 'Over the stile,' should be very faintly played in the orchestra.

Extract from Chapter I of *Curly and the Persian* by Mary Brigid Pearse

Chapter I

'The Meeting'

> Little Pussy by the fire – she was very fair. A little Dog came passing by, saying, 'Pussy, are you there? What shall we do, Pussy, what shall we do? I'll go seek my fortune and then I'll marry you.'
>
> Old Nursery Rhyme

Splash!

Splosh!

A tiny kitten and a brown, silken-haired pup were flung ruthlessly into the middle of a dirty pond where they sank immediately. Soon their squirming bodies rose to the surface of the muddy water. The kitten made one futile effort to save itself; then sank again, helplessly. The pup, however, was made of sterner stuff. To his surprise he found that he could swim quite easily, for being a water dog, he could of course, swim by instinct. So he struck out gamely for the opposite bank shaking the heavy drops from his beautiful soft brown eyes.

'Woof!' he yapped, joyously; 'I'm not drowned, after all!' Then he suddenly caught sight of the kitten's small body coming to the surface for the second time.

The pup, who had an inquiring mind, peered eagerly at the unusual floating object.

'Woof!' he cried. 'What can that queer thing be? This wants looking into, Mr Curly Tail-Wagger.' The pup had cultivated the cheery habit of talking to himself, in case he might feel lonely.

He swam over to the mysterious object; but to his surprise, just as he was about to seize it, it sank out of sight.

'Whiskers on the moon!' ejaculated the pup; 'It's gone!'

He paddled about for a time and presently it reappeared in a different place altogether.

'Woof! Woof!' barked the pup, much displeased. 'This is most annoying! I feel I must fish that thing from the water, yet I can't stay here all the evening as the water happens to be extremely wet!' He began to swim towards the bank, being too young to understand that water would not harm his beautiful feathery tail of which he was exceedingly proud. 'It must be a weasel, which keeps popping up,' he pondered. 'I used to hear old Danny singing "Pop goes the Weasel." At least give a fellow a chance to catch you!' he scolded, swimming hard across the pond. 'You're like a silly cork, popping up out of a soda water bottle!' He had almost reached the kitten when it began to sing again. But the pup's blood was up! He suddenly felt a super dog – determined not to be balked. 'The cheek of it!' he growled; 'Yah – a – a! I'll get you this time! And as the little body sank once more the gallant pup dived after it and caught it most adroitly. Then with his sleek head well up, his puppy heart swelling with pride he swam vigorously to the bank and scrambled nimbly out of the water. Laying the kitten gently on the ground he began to run wildly round and around in circles.

'Whoopsie!' he barked, joyously; 'I'm a super dog! I've saved something. It's a kitten, I do believe. Maybe it will play with me!' He raced over back to the kitten, which lay very still and cold, half dead. But Curly, who was a wise pup, knew quite well what to do. He sank down on the ground, with a front paw each side of the small, wet body, and began to lick back heat and life into it with his warm soft tongue.

Presently the kitten began to revive a little, and Curly licked harder than ever; and after a while the kitten opened one eye.

'Where am I?' she mewed, very faintly.

'You're here,' whooped Curly.

'But where's here?' she whimpered.

The pup considered this question.

'Well, I should think it's where there isn't,' he stated, gravely.

The kitten struggled to sit up and sneezed twice.

'I – I don't understand,' she said, feebly. 'Do you?'

'Of course not,' bubbled Curly; 'but it doesn't matter, does it, where we are so long as we are somewhere?'

The kitten sneezed again, and whimpered; 'I'm hungry! are you?'

'Of course I am, let's eat.'

'What shall we eat?' wailed the kitten.

'Food,' was the prompt reply.

'But where can we get food?' almost wept the poor kitten who was very sick and miserable.

'I know a fine place,' said Curly, wisely. 'Put your right paw foremost and I'll bring you to a lovely farm place where a friend of mine lives. He's a big, big, BIG horse, called Dobbin.'

'Is he a nice kind of horse to know?' asked the kitten, as she began to trot after her companion. 'I'm a very well-bred cat, myself, you know.' 'I don't know,' said Curly, light-heartedly.

'But you're not a cat – you're a kitten, aren't you?'

'My family is exceedingly well-bred,' said the kitten, arching her tiny neck; 'We are quite aristocratic, being Persians.'

'What's that?' asked the pup, his tongue lolling out in surprise.

'What's what?'

'Er – rhas – er – oh, what you said?' coughed the pup.

'It means distinguished,' said the kitten. 'But if you don't mind, I – I – think I'm going to faint!'

'I do mind,' said the pup, greatly concerned. 'I say, you know, don't do that,' he added, as the kitten fell over sideways, and staggered.

'I feel frightfully weak,' wailed the kitten.

'I know – ride on my back!' chanted Curly, triumphantly. Very gratefully the kitten crept up on the pup's warm back, taking great care not to let her claws from their sheath.

'NOW we're all right!' beamed Curly, beginning to canter quite quickly.

'We'll be at the farm in no time.'

Sure enough they arrived there very soon, and met a string of cattle which were going to the milking sheds.

'We're in splendid time,' whispered Curly, all excitement.

'Would you mind telling me who you are and where you came from?' asked the pup, as he sprang over a rabbit hole. 'We've never been properly introduced yet.'

'We can't be properly introduced now, either,' mewed the kitten clinging on to her cosy seat. 'You see, I've forgotten my name, and I'm not sure where I came from! All I do know is that I'm a white, Persian.'

'WHITE!' repeated the astonished pup, stopping so suddenly that the kitten lost her hold and flew right over her erratic steed's head into a soft heap of decayed leaves.

'Meaio – o – u!' she shrieked; 'I'm dying – I'm dead! Meai – o – u!'

The pup dashed to her rescue once more.

'Oh, I say!' he barked, 'I am sorry! I quite forgot you were riding me. I hope you are all right!'

'ALL right!' spluttered the indignant kitten. 'Would you be all right if you were flung right into a heap of dirt?'

'They are nice, soft leaves,' expostulated Curly.

'Nice!' squealed the kitten, 'NICE! Try them yourself, and find out how NICE they are!'

'Certainly,' said Curly, and he obligingly jumped into the middle of the leaves, which flew up around him. 'Yap! Ya – a – p' he shrilled; 'They are simply lovely!' And he began rolling about on his back in delight.

'DO come and have some fun,' he barked.

'I will not!' stamped the kitten with her blue eyes glaring and all her toes well out from their sheathes. 'You're a nasty big boob – that's what you are! You threw me off your back and –'

'I didn't throw you!' contradicted Curly, still rolling about.

'You did!'

'I didn't, didn't, DIDN'T!' chanted Curly. 'If you had stopped when I stopped you wouldn't have fallen off my back!'

'How did I know that you were going to stop so suddenly?' spluttered the kitten, reasonably enough.

The pup sat up with the leaves sticking all over him.

'You couldn't know, of course,' he allowed; 'as far as that goes I didn't know myself.'

The kitten stopped stamping about and suddenly began to cry, for her nerves were all on edge because of what she had gone through.

'We're a nice pair!' she wept. 'I don't know who I am, and you don't know what you are doing! Oh, dear me! Whatever shall we do?'

'I'm really awfully sorry you were so frightened,' said Curly penitently.

'Do come with me to the farm and get some hot, fresh milk. That will compose your poor nerves.'

'I'm – I'm – I'm – all of a dither!' wailed the tired kitten.

'What's that?' inquired the pup, greatly interested.

'It's the way I am!' sniffed the kitten.

'Try some other way, then,' advised the pup, jumping off the heap of leaves and lolling out his tongue, with his head on one side and one ear drooping.

He looked so drole and his voice was so coaxing that the kitten's anger vanished. Besides, she was really fond of the gallant pup who had besaved her and befriended her. So she stopped crying and smiled instead. The pup was enchanted.

'That's the ticket,' he said, gleefully. 'Will you ride again?'

'Oh – er – er – ho – I'd rather walk – if it's not too far,' she hastily decided. 'Thank you all the same.'

'But about this colour business,' began Curly as he jogged along, the kitten trotting beside him. 'You were joking, of course, when you said you are white?'

'I wasn't joking – and I am white!' squeaked the kitten, getting excited again. 'Can't you see I'm white?'

'Well, no – I – I can't say that I can!' chortled the pup. 'You look black and grey – sort of piebald, you know!'

'Oh dear me! What shall I do!' squealed the kitten. 'I was – I am a lovely creamy white all over, and –'

'All under, I should think,' said Curly, scrutinising his companion.

'Oh, dear, oh dear, whatever shall I do!' cried the kitten, wringing her tiny paws.

'Don't do that!' entreated the pup. 'You'll hurt yourself!'

'Oh, my lovely creamy fur, what has happened to it?' shrieked the kitten.

'Don't get yourself all worked up like that,' counselled the pup. 'It's bad for you, I'm certain.'

'I will!' shrieked the kitten, 'I will get excited, if I like!'

'Well, well, whatever you like yourself, of course,' said the pup. 'I was the loveliest kitten ever seen!' yelped the kitten. 'What's happened to me?'

'Personally, I should say you've got dirty,' said the pup, critically.

'A little soap and water might work wonders with you.'

'I hate soap and water!' she shuddered. 'My fur used to be brushed with a real hair brush and fine, sweet-smelling powder.'

'I say – how peculiar,' whistled the pup. 'Now, I'd prefer water – nice clean water – not that dirty pond stuff –'

'Don't mention the pond to me!' shrilled the kitten, her beautiful eyes blazing. 'I hate the pond – I'd – I'd kill it if I could!'

'Well you couldn't – so what's the use in talking?' argued Curly.

'My fur!' mewed the kitten suddenly beginning to run around crazily.

'My beautiful, creamy fur –'

'I say,' remarked Curly; 'Do you really forget you name? I –'

'Ruined!' raved the kitten; 'All ruined and destroyed!'

'Do try and remember your name?' implored Curly, 'It's so awkward when one is engaged in conversation not knowing the name of –'

'I can't remember my name!' squealed the kitten. 'The fright I got in that – you know – what – made me forget it!'

'Which?' queried Curly.

'Which what?'

'Which made you forget what?' said Curly – 'I don't quite understand!' The kitten positively hissed with annoyance.

'The – the – WHAT YOU KNOW – made me forget my name!' she shrieked; 'I'll never – never – never – never – NEVER –'

'Easy on!' warned Curly, suddenly beginning to run round in circles after his own tail; 'You're getting all worked up again, aren't you?'

'Meiao – aow – H!' spluttered the kitten.

'Why ever did you go into the pond?' asked Curly as he snapped at his tail and fell over backwards.

'I didn't go into it!' spluttered the indignant kitten.

'Why did you fall in, then?'

'I didn't fall into it!' stamped the kitten.

'Oh, I'm beginning to understand,' barked Curly. 'Someone shoved you in.'

'Someone THREW me in!' shrieked the kitten. 'Threw me – right – in – SPLASH!'

'Woof! Woof!' cried Curly, spinning round quicker than ever. 'So I was thrown in! RIGHT IN! SPLOSH!'

The kitten began stamping up and down again, its back arched and its tail erect, while its eyes glared.

'Yah – a – azeen!' it yelped. 'Zaa – sph – zaa – ah!'

'I quite agree with you!' yapped Curly.

'Why were you thrown into – you know where?' asked the kitten.

The pup stopped running around in circles, and became very grave.

'I think it was because of a horrid thing called Licence,' he said, cautiously.

'What's that?'

'Well, it's some sort of a thing that crops up every year,' returned the pup, rather puzzled.

'What sort of a thing is it?' demanded the kitten, anxiously. 'Does it bite, or push animals into – you know what?'

'No – no – no! It doesn't do just that,' returned Curly, slowly. 'But it seems to make people want to throw stray dogs and puppies out or even drown them.'

'How horrible!' shivered the kitten.

'Shocking! They are like bits of paper, and sometimes they are pushed in the letter boxes by postmen.'

'They are cruel,' moaned the kitten.

'I think it's the people who are cruel,' said Curly, thoughtfully; 'when the Licence comes along people who don't really care for dogs just throw them out, or make them into sausages.'

'How do you know so much when you are only a puppy?' the kitten wanted to know.

'I had a friend once,' explained Curly, 'a wise, old Shepherd dog, called Faithful. He knew everything worth knowing, and he used to tell me things, dear old Faithful!' and the pup sighed deeply.

'Is he sick, or has anything happened to him?' asked the kitten, kindly.

'I don't know where he is,' admitted Curly, regretfully; 'he was sent away from the farm we're going to now, because a new head cattle man said he was getting too slow to herd the sheep properly.'

'What a shame,' mewed the kitten.

'It was cruel!' exclaimed Curly, indignantly. 'The nice stable lads and the two young masters were furious, but I was no use. Faithful was simply pushed!'

'And he told you all about this Licence business?' observed the kitten.

'Sure,' said Curly. 'If Mr Licence is not satisfied it's all up with us dogs.'

'How do you mean, up with you?' asked the kitten, staring at him, quite puzzled. 'It was all down with you, wasn't it?'

The pup chuckled.

'You're right,' he agreed; 'but I was only using a figure of speech that time.'

'What is a figure of speech?' persisted the kitten, who was a very sensible little cat and wanted to learn all she could.

'Well – er – what I said was a figure of speech,' blurted out Curly, who was a little puzzled himself. 'If you understand?'

'I certainly do not understand, and neither do you!' squealed the kitten.

'Well, it doesn't really matter, anyhow,' said Curly, anxious to change the subject. 'Have you noticed my tail, by any chance? It's the loveliest thing – all feathery!' and he waved it vigorously in the air. The kitten flew at it, with a squeak of delight.

'It's just dinky!' she crooned, beginning to play with and frisk with the gracefully waving tail.

'Glad you like it,' said Curly, greatly flattered. 'Notice the sweet curl in it – that's why I'm called Curly, you know.'

'Purr – er – r – r – !' crooned the kitten.

'Let's have fun,' suggested Curly, and he started to run with the kitten chasing after his waving tail. They rushed along until they came to a big garden which surrounded a fine tall house. The garden gate was open so the pup and the kitten tore in and began frolicking all about a nice green plot of grass. At one of the upper windows of the big house a white-faced little girl looked down in rapt enjoyment at the frisking animals.

'Just like a bit of feathery fluff, my tail!' barked Curly.

The kitten uttered a sudden shriek and tumbled head over heels which startled Curly so much that he too, turned a summersault, and the two animals came back to earth face to face both staring at each other in a most surprised manner.

'I've found it!' shrieked the kitten, so suddenly that Curly rolled over on his back with shock. 'Well, keep it, whatever it is!' he yapped. 'But do, please, try not to be so sudden! It upsets a fellow. You'll give me the jigs in a minute.'

'Harooh!' squeaked the kitten, waltzing about on its hind legs, in wild excitement. 'I've remembered my name! You said it –'

'I couldn't!' protested Curly. 'I don't know it, and –'

'You said "Fluffy"!' mewed the kitten, still dancing crazily. 'And my name is FLUFFS! I remember everything now!'

ENDNOTES

Introduction

1. Letter from James Pearse to Margaret Brady (n.d.), MS 21082/6, National Library of Ireland (NLI).
2. Mary Brigid Pearse, *The Home-Life of Pádraig Pearse* (Dublin: Browne and Nolan, 1934), p. 15.
3. Margaret Pearse, 'St Enda's', *Capuchin Annual* (1942), 227.

Chapter 1

1. Pearse, *The Home-Life*, p. 23.
2. Margaret Pearse, 'Foreword', *Cuimhní na bPiarsach: Memories of the Brothers Pearse* (Dublin: Brothers Pearse Commemoration Committee, 1958), 3.
3. Letter from Fr Pius Devine, Passionist Order, Holy Cross Monastery, Belfast, to James Pearse (26 December 1877), MS 21077/2, NLI.
4. Róisín Ní Ghairbhí, *16 Lives: Willie Pearse* (Dublin: O'Brien Press, 2015), p. 26.
5. Letter from James Pearse to Margaret Brady (n.d.), MS 21082/6, NLI.
6. Letter from James Pearse to Margaret Brady (n.d.), MS 21082/8, NLI.
7. Letter from James Pearse to Margaret Brady (n.d.), MS 21082/9, NLI.
8. Letter from James Pearse to Margaret Brady (n.d.), MS 21082/6, NLI.
9. Letter from James Pearse to Margaret Brady (n.d.), MS 21082/10, NLI.
10. Pearse, *The Home-Life*, p. 60.
11. Ibid., p. 20.
12. Ibid., p. 26.
13. Ibid.
14. Ibid., p. 22.
15. Margaret Pearse, 'Patrick and Willie Pearse', *Capuchin Annual* (1943), 86.
16. Pearse, *The Home-Life*, p. 25.
17. Ibid., p. 30.
18. Ibid., p. 60.
19. Ibid., p. 31. This album later found a new life as Mary Brigid's much-beloved music case.
20. Obituary notice of Sr Bridget of the Holy Trinity of the Incarnate Word and Blessed Sacrament (Emily McGloughlin, eldest daughter of Emily and

Alfred). She entered the convent of the Incarnate Word and Blessed Sacrament, Brownsville, Texas on 14 December 1901 and was professed on 26 July 1903. She taught at primary level, played the organ, taught music and was assistant superior. We are grateful to Sr Marian Bradley, Sr Brenda Thompson and Sr Rose Miriam Gansle of the Sisters of the Incarnate Word and Blessed Sacrament, Texas, USA for this information.

21. Letter from James Pearse to Margaret Brady (n.d.), MS 21082/13, NLI.
22. Letter from James Pearse to Margaret Brady (n.d.), MS 21082/14, NLI.
23. Letter from James Pearse to Margaret Brady (n.d.), MS 21082/15, NLI.
24. Letter from James Pearse to Margaret Brady (n.d.), MS 21082/11, NLI.
25. Pearse, *The Home-Life*, p. 38.
26. Louis N. Le Roux and Desmond Ryan, *Patrick H. Pearse* (Dublin: Talbot Press, 1932), p. 6.
27. Pearse, *The Home-Life*, p. 33.
28. Ibid., p. 34.
29. Ibid., p. 80.
30. Ibid.
31. Ibid., p. 84.
32. Ibid.
33. Ibid., p. 86.
34. Ibid., p. 56.
35. Ibid., p. 74.
36. Ibid., p. 64.
37. Ibid., p. 97.
38. Pearse, 'Patrick and Willie Pearse', 87.
39. Pearse, *The Home-Life*, p. 70.
40. Ibid., p. 79.
41. Ibid., p. 52.
42. Ibid., p. 55.
43. Ibid., p. 86.
44. Ibid., p. 58.
45. Ibid., p. 15.

Chapter 2

1. Pearse, *The Home-Life*, p. 14.
2. Margaret Pearse, 'Happy memories', *Centenary Magazine of the Holy Faith Sisters* (1967), 66.
3. This needlework set is on display at the Pearse Museum, St Enda's, Rathfarnham, Dublin.
4. 'Notes on Miss Margaret Pearse', Holy Faith Sisters Congregational Archives, Glasnevin, Dublin (n.d.), 2.
5. Pearse, 'Happy memories', 66.
6. Ibid., 69.
7. Ní Ghairbhí, *Willie Pearse*, p. 43.
8. Ibid.

9. Pearse, *The Home-Life*, p. 112.
10. Ibid., p. 104.
11. Ibid., p. 118.
12. Ruth Dudley Edwards, *Patrick Pearse: The Triumph of Failure* (Dublin: Irish Academic Press, 2006), p. 6.
13. Pearse, 'Patrick and Willie Pearse', 86.
14. Pearse, *The Home-Life*, p. 109.
15. 'New Ireland Literary Society', *Freeman's Journal (FJ)* (19 January 1897), 7.
16. 'New Ireland Literary Society', *FJ* (1 March 1898), 3.
17. Ní Ghairbhí, *Willie Pearse*, p. 46.
18. 'New Ireland Literary Society', *FJ* (16 October 1897), 5.
19. Dudley Edwards, *Patrick Pearse*, p. 17
20. Pearse, *The Home-Life*, p. 117.
21. Ibid.
22. Ibid.
23. Mary Colum, *Life and the Dream* (Dublin: Dolmen Press, 1966), p. 133.
24. Pearse, *The Home-Life*, p. 78.
25. Ibid.
26. Ibid., p. 127.
27. Dudley Edwards, *Patrick Pearse*, p. 24.
28. See Mary Louise O'Donnell, 'Owen Lloyd and the de-anglicization of the Irish harp', *Éire-Ireland,* 48, nos 3 and 4 (Fall/Winter 2013), 155–75.
29. *An Claidheamh Soluis (ACS)* (20 January 1900), 715.
30. *ACS* (24 February 1900), 790.
31. *Connradh na Gaedhilge–Programme of the Oireachtas or Irish Literary Festival, Round Room, Rotunda, May 1898* (Dublin: Gaelic League, 1898), 10.
32. O'Donnell, 'Owen Lloyd and the de-anglicization of the Irish harp', 168.
33. Patrick also acquired a Grecian Érard concert harp for Mary Brigid. In 1950, Margaret donated this harp to the community of the Sisters of the Infant Jesus, Drishane, Millstreet, Co. Cork. Margaret visited the convent on many occasions as one of the sisters attended St Ita's/Scoil Íde. When the convent closed, the sisters donated this harp to the Cork School of Music in 1992. We are grateful to Sr Rosemary Barter, provincial of the Infant Jesus Sisters, Cork, for this information.
34. 'The Late Mr. James Pearse', *FJ* (10 September 1900), 6.

Chapter 3

1. Margaret Pearse, 'Patrick and Willie Pearse', 87.
2. *ACS* (24 November 1906, 7 & 11 May 1907, 7).
3. *ACS* (23 December 1905), 4.
4. *ACS* (24 November 1906), 5.
5. Pearse, *The Home-Life*, p. 140.
6. Pearse, 'Patrick and Willie Pearse', 87.
7. Desmond Ryan, *The Story of a Success by P.H. Pearse* (Dublin & London: Maunsel, 1918), p. 11.

8. Ibid., p. 6.
9. Ibid., p. 47.
10. Dudley Edwards, *Patrick Pearse*, p. 120.
11. Kenneth Reddin, 'A Man called Pearse', *Studies: An Irish Quarterly Review*, 34, no. 134 (June 1945), 244.
12. Personal correspondence by the authors with Fr Joseph Mallin SJ, Wah Yan Jesuit College, Hong Kong.
13. Ní Ghairbhí, *Willie Pearse*, p. 119.
14. Ryan, *The Story of a Success*, p. 21. Alfred's mother Emily worked as a midwife in various parts of Ireland, including Fanad, Co. Donegal. From the 1920s, Emily lived in Emmet's Fort, one of the lodges at St Enda's, and died there in 1945.
15. Pearse, *The Home-Life*, p. 75.
16. Ibid.
17. *Prospectus for St Ita's/Sgoil Íde (1910–11)*, p. 5.
18. Colum, *Life and the Dream,* p. 134.
19. Pearse, *The Home-Life*, pp. 152–3.
20. Ibid., p. 153.
21. Ibid., pp. 155–6.
22. 'The passion play at the Abbey', *FJ* (7 April 1911), 8.
23. 'Plays at the Abbey Theatre', *Irish Independent (II)* (27 December 1911), 6.
24. Ibid.
25. 'Leinster Stage Society', *Evening Herald* (24 February 1911), 4.
26. Ibid.
27. 'Leinster Stage Society', *Irish Times (IT)* (6 February 1912), 6.
28. Ibid.
29. Desmond Ryan, 'Margaret Pearse', *Capuchin Annual* (1942), 316.
30. Obituary Notice of Mrs Margaret Pearse, MS 21092, NLI.

Chapter 4

1. Margaret Pearse, 'St Enda's', *Capuchin Annual* (1942), 229.
2. Pearse, *The Home-Life*, p. 121.
3. Mary Brigid Pearse, *A Visit to Rosmuc with Patrick Pearse*, Pearse Museum and St Enda's at Kilmainham Gaol (PMSTE), 1.
4. Ibid.
5. Ibid., 2.
6. Ibid., 5.
7. *An Barr Buadh* (5 April 1912).
8. Brendan Walsh, *The Pedagogy of Protest* (Bern: Lang, 2007), p. 269.
9. The students included Fintan Murphy, Éamonn Bulfin, Frank Burke, Bryan Joyce, John J. Kilgallon, Conor and Eunan McGinley, Desmond Ryan and Joe Sweeney, all members of 'E' Company, 4th Batallion, Dublin Brigade, stationed at the GPO during the Rising.
10. Pearse, 'St Enda's', 227.

11. Margaret Pearse, 'The last days of Pat and Willie Pearse at St Enda's', *Leabhrán Cuimhneacháin arna bronnadh ar Ócáid Bronnadh Eochair Scoil Éanna as Uachtarán na hÉireann Éamon de Valera 23 Aibreán 1970* (Dublin: Office of Public Works, 1970), 38.

12. Ibid.

13. Pearse, 'St Enda's', 227.

14. Michael Foley, *The Bloodied Field: Croke Park, Sunday 21 November 1920* (Dublin: O'Brien Press, 2014), p. 130.

15. 'The Ceannt papers: dead march in a garden before the Rising', *Irish Press* (*IP*) (11 January 1949), 6.

16. Pearse, 'St Enda's' and 'The last days of Pat and Willie Pearse at St Enda's'.

17. Pearse, 'St Enda's', 227.

18. Ibid., 228.

19. Ibid.

20. Pearse, 'The last days of Pat and Willie Pearse at St Enda's', 39.

21. Ibid.

22. Pearse, 'St Enda's', 229.

23. Dudley Edwards, *Patrick Pearse*, p. 277 and fn 3, p. 359.

24. Pearse, 'St Enda's', 229. Margaret stated that Patrick had requested that Fr Aloysius relate the news of his death to his mother and sister after his execution.

25. Ibid.

26. Prior to the Easter Rising, Kilmainham Gaol (opened in 1796) had been closed since 1910. However, it was reopened at Easter 1916 to accommodate the hundreds of men and women arrested for their participation in the Rising.

27. Pearse, 'St Enda's', 230.

28. Thomas Kent was executed in Cork on 9 May 1916 and Roger Casement was hanged in Pentonville Gaol, London, on 3 August. The remaining men sentenced to death had their sentences commuted to penal servitude ranging from three years to life.

29. Helen Litton (ed.), *Kathleen Clarke: Revolutionary Woman* (Dublin: O'Brien Press, 2008), p. 141.

30. Letter from Bishop Edward Thomas O'Dwyer to General John Grenfell Maxwell (17 May 1916), http://letters1916.maynoothuniversity.ie/ diyhistory/items/show/2111 (accessed 5 July 2016).

31. Pearse, 'St Enda's', 227.

32. Ibid., 230.

33. Joseph McGrath was the first secretary of the INAVDF. He resigned as the prisoners were being released and was replaced by Michael Collins on 19 February 1917.

34. Litton, *Kathleen Clarke*, p. 176.

35. Witness statement of Seán O'Duffy, WS 618, Bureau of Military History (BMH).

36. Letter from Eugene Cronin to Margaret Pearse (12 July 1916), PMSTE.

37. Letter from Margaret Pearse to Eugene Cronin (12 July 1916), PMSTE.
38. Letter from Fr Eugene Nevin to Mrs Pearse (19 May 1916), MS 21059/2/6, NLI.
39. Witness Statement of Desmond Ryan, WS 725, BMH.
40. Letter from Mrs Pearse to Fr Moclan (2 March 1920), MS 21059/19/27, NLI.
41. 'Cullenswood house raid', *FJ* (10 March 1921), 6.
42. 'Violation of Pádraig Pearse's home: Mrs. Pearse's words to the Free State soldiers' (1922), MS 17476/1/23, NLI.
43. Ibid.
44. Letter from Margaret Pearse to Mr and Mrs McGrath (17 March 1927), PMSTE.
45. Draft letter from Mrs Pearse to the secretary of the Ministry of Defence (24 April 1928), MS 21059/20/9, NLI.
46. Letter from Fr Denis Fahey to Margaret Pearse (1928), PMSTE.
47. Letter from Ernest Blythe to Mrs Pearse (10 August 1931), National Archives of Ireland (NAI).
48. Letter from Maurice Moynihan (private secretary to Éamon de Valera) to Mrs Pearse (July 1932), NAI.
49. Walsh, *The Pedagogy of Protest*, p. 325.
50. 'Students' visit: interest in modern newspaper plant', *IP* (17 September 1931), 1.
51. Personal correspondence by the authors with Fr Joseph Mallin, Hong Kong.

Chapter 5

1. Note from Mary Brigid to her mother (1924), PMSTE.
2. *The Cross* 7, no. 7, 164.
3. 'Advertisement', *Irish Independent* (9 July 1917), 4.
4. Mary Brigid Pearse, *The Murphys of Ballystack* (Dublin: M.H. Gill, 1917), p. 19.
5. Ibid., p. 57.
6. Dudley Edwards, *Patrick Pearse*, p. 167.
7. *The Tablet* (6 October 1917) 130, no. 4039, 430.
8. Letter from Appleton-Century Company, London to Mary Brigid Pearse (14 July 1936), PMSTE.
9. Letter from N.G. Craig to Mary Brigid Pearse (20 July 1936), PMSTE.
10. Mary Brigid Pearse, 'The life of Pádraig Pearse', *Our Boys*, 12, no. 15 (15 April 1926), 628.
11. 'Devotion to national cause', *IP* (23 April 1932), 1.
12. 'Late Mrs. M. Pearse', *IP* (24 April 1933), 5.
13. 'Death of Mrs. Pearse', *II* (23 April 1932), 9.
14. 'Margaret Pearse', *IP* (23 April 1932), 8.
15. 'To hold what they upheld', *IP* (27 April 1932), 1.
16. Éamon de Valera, 'Panegyric', *Capuchin Annual* (1942), 336.

17. 'Provision in will of Mrs Pearse', *IP* (11 March 1933), 1.
18. Thomas H. Kinane, *The Angel of the Altar: or the Love of the Most Adorable and Most Sacred Heart of Jesus* (Dublin: M.H. Gill, n.d.), PMSTE.
19. Letter from Bernard Bernstein to Daniel C. Maher (9 April 1934), PMSTE.
20. Record of meeting between Bernard Bernstein and Daniel C. Maher (19 April 1934), PMSTE.
21. Letter from Bernard Bernstein to Daniel C. Maher (28 March 1935), PMSTE.
22. Record of meeting between Daniel C. Maher and Bernard Bernstein (10 December 1934), PMSTE.
23. Letter from C. O'Hassell (Manager at Eason booksellers) to Mrs Cruise O'Brien (23 December 1935), PMSTE.
24. Letter from Robert Eason to Mary Brigid Pearse (6 January 1936), PMSTE.
25. Letter from Fr Joseph Smith to Mary Brigid Pearse (16 February 1935), PMSTE.
26. *Evening Herald* (9 September 1935), 3 and *Irish Examiner* (*IE*) (9 September 1935), 10.
27. Letter from Bernard Bernstein to Mary Brigid Pearse (12 November 1935), PMSTE.
28. Ibid.
29. Letter from Mary Brigid Pearse to Bernard Bernstein (n.d.), PMSTE.
30. Pearse, *The Home-Life*, p. 6.
31. Ibid., p. 7.
32. Ibid., p. 15.
33. Ibid., p. 13.
34. Ibid., p. 14.
35. Ibid., p. 15.
36. Ibid., p. 26.
37. Ibid., p. 48.
38. Ibid., p. 60.
39. Ibid., p. 138.
40. Ibid., p. 68.
41. 'The home life of Pádraig Pearse', *IE* (6 March 1935), 4.
42. Letter from Fr Francis Farrell to Mary Brigid Pearse (10 June 1936), PMSTE.
43. Dudley Edwards, *Patrick Pearse*, p. 328.
44. Ibid., p. 120.
45. Letter from Fr Joseph Smith to Margaret Pearse (14 November 1947) and letter from Mary Murphy to Margaret Pearse (6 December 1949), PMSTE.

Chapter 6

1. Notes on Miss Margaret Pearse, Holy Faith Sisters Congregational Archives (HFSCA), 3.
2. 'The same old fight, Miss Pearse and family aspirations', *IP* (19 January 1933), 2.

3. Fianna Fáil were one seat short of an overall majority in the general election of 24 January 1933.
4. 'Miss Pearse recalls an interview', *IP* (28 June 1937), 12.
5. Diarmaid Ferriter, *The Transformation of Ireland 1900–2000* (London: Profile Books, 2005), p. 369.
6. 'A declaration of independence', *IP* (29 June 1937), 13.
7. 'Women cheer Miss Pearse', *IP* (21 June 1937), 10.
8. The County Dublin Constituency was reduced from an eight-seater in 1933 to a five-seater for the 1937 election.
9. 'Women candidates for the Senate', *IP* (16 March 1938), 5.
10. General circular for Seanad elections (8 June 1954), PMSTE.
11. 'A declaration of independence', *IP* (29 June 1937), 13.
12. Seanad Éireann Debates, 36, no. 3 (15 December 1948), http://oireachtasdebates.oireachtas.ie/debates%20authoring/debateswebpack.nsf/takes/seanad1948121500004?opendocument (accessed 4 June 2016).
13. 'Day of re-union coming', *Fermanagh Herald* (23 June 1945), 8.
14. Ibid.
15. Ibid.
16. 'Miss Pearse at home in Tyrone', *IP* (20 February 1950), 5.
17. 'Language will remain lost if lost now', *IP* (12 October 1950), 7.
18. Éamonn de Barra, 'A valiant woman', *Capuchin Annual* (1969), 56.
19. 'Father Mathew feis opens', *IP* (6 April 1953), 11.
20. de Barra, 'A valiant woman', 53.
21. 'Speak Irish, says senator', *IP* (27 April 1953), 9.
22. *Prospectus for St Enda's/Sgoil Éanna (1908–09).*
23. Dudley Edwards, *Patrick Pearse,* p. 333.
24. 'Returned Pearse's letters', *IP* (24 September 1946), 5.
25. 'The Pearse papers', *Ulster Herald* (24 August 1946), 4.
26. 'Pearse's Speech', *IT* (15 July 1969), 11.
27. 'Women candidates for the Senate', *IP* (16 March 1938), 5.
28. Letter from Margaret Pearse to An Taoiseach Éamon de Valera (13 October 1941), NAI.
29. Letter from Margaret Pearse to Fr Senan Moynihan (1 December 1942), MS 8265/105 and letter from Office of County Commissioner, Dublin to Fr Senan Moynihan (24 March 1943), MS 8265/118, Trinity College Dublin.
30. Notes on Miss Margaret Pearse, 1 & 3 (HFSCA).
31. Margaret Pearse, *How to Serve Mass, with Liturgical Prayers from the Missal* (Irish Messenger: Dublin, 1947), p. 4.
32. Thomas MacGreevy, 'Jubilate', *Capuchin Annual* (1950), 162.
33. Margaret Pearse, 'Memories of our pilgrimage', *Capuchin Annual* (1950), 177.
34. Ibid., 173.
35. Ibid., 178.
36. Ibid., 180.

37. 'Obituary notice of Fr. Gerald O'Boyle', *The Cross* 47 (1956–7), 203. We are grateful to Fr Brian Mulcahy, archivist of the Passionist Community, Mount Argus, Dublin, for this information.

38. Ibid. Fr O'Boyle's penitents came from diverse backgrounds and from all parts of Ireland, they included Éamon de Valera, Dr Patrick Dunne, the Bishop of Nara, 'priests and religious, professional men and politicians, working men and housewives'. Ibid.

39. de Barra, 'A valiant woman', 56.

40. 'A worthy appeal – plea by Miss M. Pearse', *II* (10 June 1938), 12.

41. 'Senator Pearse honoured', *IP* (11 January 1965), 3.

42. Letter from Margaret Pearse to Desmond Ryan (22 October 1954), LA10/192, Desmond Ryan Papers, University College Dublin Archives.

43. de Barra, 'A valiant woman', 55.

44. Ibid.

45. 'Miss Pearse's plea to voters', *IP* (2 October 1961), 4.

46. 'Plea for Irish at mealtimes', *II* (12 November 1962), 1.

47. 'I feel so bitter about St Enda's', *Sunday Independent* (26 April 1970), 24.

48. 'Future of Pearse home unknown', *II* (11 March 1966), 14.

49. 'Future of Pearse property', *IE* (23 March 1966), 2.

50. The relatives of Seán MacDiarmada did not attend the official commemorations of the Rising and marked the occasion with an alternative commemoration in Kiltyclogher, Co. Leitrim, organised by the National Graves Association.

51. de Barra, 'A valiant woman', 56.

52. *IP* (19 September 1966), 14.

53. Letters to the editor', *IP* (14 February 1967), 7.

54. See *IP* (23 March 1967, 1 & 27 March 1967, 3).

55. 'Senator Margaret Pearse (90) dies in Dublin', *II* (8 November 1968), 3.

56. 'Senator Pearse celebrates her 89th birthday', *II* (5 August 1967), 9.

57. 'Senator Margaret Pearse dies at 90', *IT* (8 November 1968), 13.

58. 'Margaret Pearse first Irishwoman to get State funeral', *II* (11 November 1968), 7.

59. 'Senator Margaret Pearse (90) dies in Dublin', *II* (8 November 1968), 3.

60. 'Margaret Pearse's Graveside Oration by Jack Lynch' (1968), NAI.

61. 'She remembered charities', *IP* (22 March 1969), 3.

62. 'Nation takes over Pearse school', *IT* (24 April 1970), 13.

Conclusion

1. Pearse, *The Home-Life*, pp. 165–6.

2. Letter from unidentified sister from the Convent of the Sacred Heart, Roscrea, Co. Tipperary to Margaret Pearse (August 1968), PMSTE.

3. Note on Miss Margaret M. Pearse (n.d.), NAI.

SELECT BIBLIOGRAPHY

Archives and collections

Archive of the Passionist Community, Mount Argus, Dublin
Archive of the Sisters of the Incarnate Word and Blessed Sacrament, Texas, USA
Bureau of Military History (BMH)
Desmond Ryan Papers, University College Dublin Archives
Papers of Patrick Henry Pearse and his family in the Fr Senan Moynihan Collection, Manuscripts Department, Trinity College Dublin (TCD)
Holy Faith Sisters Congregational Archives, Glasnevin, Dublin (HFSCA)
Irish Capuchin Provincial Archives, Church Street, Dublin
Pearse Museum and St Enda's Collections at Kilmainham Gaol (PMSTE)
National Archives of Ireland, Dublin (NAI)
Pearse Family Papers, National Library of Ireland, Dublin (NLI)

Articles, books and other documents

Augusteijn, Joost, *Patrick Pearse: The Making of a Revolutionary*. Basingstoke: Palgrave Macmillan, 2010.
Colum, Mary, *Life and the Dream*. Dublin: Dolmen Press, 1966.
Connradh na Gaedhilge–Programme of the Oireachtas or Irish Literary Festival, Round Room, Rotunda, May 1898. Dublin: Gaelic League, 1898.
Cooke, Pat, *Scéal Scoil Éanna: The Story of an Educational Adventure*. Dublin: Office of Public Works, 1986.
Crowley, Brian, *Patrick Pearse: A Life in Pictures*. Cork; Mercier Press, 2013.
Cuimhní na bPiarsach: Memories of the Brothers Pearse. Dublin: Brothers Pearse Commemoration Committee, 1958.
Cummins, Gerry and de Búrca, Éanna, *The Frank Burke Story*. Naas: Irish Print, 2016.
de Barra, Éamonn, 'A valiant woman', *Capuchin Annual* (1969): 53–6.
de Valera, Éamon, 'Panegyric', *Capuchin Annual* (1942): 336.
Dudley Edwards, Ruth, *The Triumph of Failure*. Dublin: Irish Academic Press, 2006.

Ferriter, Diarmaid, *The Transformation of Ireland 1900–2000*. London: Profile Books, 2005.

Finnegan, Thomas A., 'Pearse on Education', *The Furrow*, 4, no. 9 (September 1953): 510–16.

Foley, Michael, *The Bloodied Field: Croke Park, Sunday 21 November 1920*. Dublin: O'Brien Press, 2014.

Kinane, Thomas H., *The Angel of the Altar: or, the Love of the Most Adorable and Most Sacred Heart of Jesus*. Dublin: M.H. Gill, n.d.

Le Roux, Louis N. and Ryan, Desmond, *Patrick H. Pearse*. Dublin: Talbot Press, 1932.

Litton, Helen (ed.), *Kathleen Clarke: Revolutionary Woman*. Dublin: O'Brien Press, 2008.

MacGreevy, Thomas, 'Jubilate', *Capuchin Annual* (1950): 161–8.

Ní Ghairbhí, Róisín, *16 Lives: Willie Pearse*. Dublin: O'Brien Press, 2015.

Nic Shiúbhlaigh, Máire, *The Splendid Years: Recollections of Máire Nic Shiúbhlaigh as told to Edward Kenny*. Dublin: Duffy, 1955.

Ó Buachalla, Séamas, *The Letters of P.H. Pearse*. Gerrards Cross: Smythe, 1980.

O'Donnell, Mary Louise, 'Owen Lloyd and the de-anglicization of the Irish harp', *Éire-Ireland*, 48, nos 3 and 4 (Fall/Winter 2013): 155–75.

O'Donnell, Ruán, *16 Lives: Patrick Pearse*. Dublin: O'Brien Press, 2016.

Ó Fearaíl, Pádraig, *The Story of Conradh na Gaeilge: A History of the Gaelic League*. Dublin: An Clodhanna Teoranta, 1975.

Pearse, James, 'A Reply to Professor Maguire's pamphlet "England's duty to Ireland" as it appears to an Englishman'. Dublin: M.H. Gill, 1886.

Pearse, Margaret, 'Foreword', *Cuimhní na bPiarsach: Memories of the Brothers Pearse* (Dublin: Brothers Pearse Commemoration Committee, 1958): 3.

– 'Happy memories', *Centenary Magazine of the Holy Faith Sisters* (1967): 66–9.

– *How to Serve Mass, with Liturgical Prayers from the Missal*. Dublin: Irish Messenger, 1947.

– 'Memories of our pilgrimage', *Capuchin Annual* (1950): 169–83.

– 'Patrick and Willie Pearse', *Capuchin Annual* (1943): 86–8.

– 'St Enda's', *Capuchin Annual* (1942): 227–30.

– 'The Last Days of Pat and Willie Pearse at St Enda's', *Leabhrán Cuimhneacháin arna bronnadh ar Ócáid Bronnadh Eochair Scoil Éanna as Uachtarán na hÉireann Éamon de Valera 23 Aibreán 1970*. Dublin: OPW, 1970.

Pearse, Mary Brigid, 'A visit to Rosmuc with Patrick Pearse (n.d.). PMSTE.

– *The Home-Life of Pádraig Pearse*. Dublin: Browne and Nolan, 1934.

– 'The life of Pádraig Pearse', *Our Boys*, 15 April 1926–20 January 1927.

– *The Murphys of Ballystack*. Dublin: M.H. Gill, 1917.

– 'Two Brothers', *Irish Press* (3 May 1940), 6.

Pearse, Patrick, *Three Lectures on Gaelic Topics*. Dublin: M.H. Gill, 1898.

Prospectus for St Enda's/Sgoil Éanna (1908–9).

Prospectus for St Ita's/Sgoil Íde (1910–11).

Reddin, Kenneth, 'A Man called Pearse', *Studies: An Irish Quarterly Review*, 34, no. 134 (June 1945): 241–51.

Ryan, Desmond, 'Margaret Pearse', *Capuchin Annual* (1942): 312–18.

– *The Story of a Success by P.H. Pearse.* Dublin & London: Maunsel, 1918.

Sisson, Elaine, *Pearse's Patriots: The Cult of Boyhood.* Cork: Cork University Press, 2004.

Walsh, Brendan, *The Pedagogy of Protest.* Bern: Lang, 2007.

Newspapers and Journals

An Barr Buadh
An Claidheamh Soluis
Capuchin Annual
Fermanagh Herald
Freeman's Journal
Irish Examiner
Irish Independent
Irish Press
Irish Times
Sunday Independent
The Cross
The Tablet
Ulster Herald

Websites

http://letters1916.maynoothuniversity.ie/diyhistory/items/show/2111 (accessed 5 July 2016)

http://oireachtasdebates.oireachtas.ie/debates%20authoring/debateswebpack.nsf/takes/seanad1948121500004?opendocument (accessed 4 June 2016)

INDEX